LIFE AFTER HAIR COLOR

By

SUSAN V. DARDEN

© 2003 by Susan V. Darden. All rights reserved.

No part of this book may be reproduced, stored in a retrieval system, or transmitted by any means, electronic, mechanical, photocopying, recording, or otherwise, without written permission from the author.

ISBN: 1-4107-9254-4 (e-book)
ISBN: 1-4107-9255-2 (Paperback)

Library of Congress Control Number: 2003096486

This book is printed on acid free paper.

Printed in the United States of America
Bloomington, IN

1stBooks – rev. 09/09/03

Table of Contents

Introduction		v
Chapter 1	The Birth of a Good Woman	1
Chapter 2	How Do You Get There From Here?	5
Chapter 3	The Law of Charlie	11
Chapter 4	Balance	15
Chapter 5	Who Was That Masked Man?	19
Chapter 6	Hunger	25
Chapter 7	Never Wear Shoes That Hurt	33
Chapter 8	Who Bought This Dress?	39
Chapter 9	The Gift That Keeps On Giving	45
Chapter 10	Jewelry	49
Chapter 11	Forgiveness	55
Chapter 12	The Wraparound	61
Chapter 13	The Staff Meeting	69
Chapter 14	Reruns	77
Chapter 15	Out of the Box	83
Chapter 16	Learning to Be a Woman	93
Chapter 17	My Porsche	101
Chapter 18	Enough	107
Chapter 19	The Kitchen Is Burning	117
Chapter 20	Living Juicy	127

Introduction

There is no shortage of books available to tell you what you are doing wrong in your life. This book will not be about that. You already know what is wrong in your life better than anyone else does. This one will be about being real. Listening to what you know, learning how to do that more often, being content with your answer, being good to yourself, and most of all cutting yourself one big break for a change. This life is not the rehearsal for something yet to come. It is the real deal. Live it like it you know that, it works much better that way.

I have been one of those individuals who could not decide what they wanted to be when they grew up. It was a good thing that I happened to be good at more than one thing so that I could survive without needing to make a final decision. I was able to bounce around a bit, sampling and testing new ground. I consider myself very fortunate. Not too long ago I realized from the very center of my being what I wanted to be once and for all. *A good woman.* I smiled the first time I thought about it, it sounds so very simple. It is one of the most challenging jobs in the world. To close your eyes each night and know that you did the best you could with what you had to work with that day, is an ambition worth having and reaps countless rewards in satisfaction, self respect and serenity. A good woman sleeps soundly and wakes up ready for a new day, confident that there is nothing she can't handle.

A good woman is soft without being a wimp; she can rise out of her pool of tears to put her arm around a friend in pain. She can state the facts of her life without flinching, because she did not run to escape the truth. A good woman knows that breaking a pinky swear will give you nose hairs and would die before she would stoop to that level. A good woman knows to go to her mother's bedside when she is in the hospital to brush her hair, because she knows her mother would do that for her. She maintains the dignity of her own spirit and celebrates that dignity in others. A good woman respects love and welcomes it into her life, but knows that it is not always enough in its own right.

If a few people think I am a good woman after I am gone, my life will have been a success. The jobs I have had, the words I have written, the houses I have lived in, the bargains I have hunted down will not matter much if I am any less. If I go without anyone else realizing I was a good woman, I will know.

I believe in the saying "what goes down, comes around." If it is not true, I do not want to know about it. It has kept me from fulfilling my revenge fantasies more than once. I have learned that living well is the best revenge. It is not possible in this life for someone to hurt your spirit without getting some pain on themselves. I have to admit, there have been times in my life when I have done the "right" thing only because I did not wish to pay the karmic consequences. Sometimes the consequences of an action are just enough to keep us in line. Whatever works. I know this to be true because I was not always of that mindset and I was the one that had someone's pain on my hands. I paid for whatever I did, and I will again, if I do harm. That is how it works. I accept that and have come to love that system. Life comes with the privilege of free will and the responsibility of choosing well. Karmic debt has a phenomenal interest rate; I prefer not to finance my soul that way.

I wrote this book with the idea that it would speak to the reader the way the realizations spoke to me. I wanted it to be a "girlfriends" book. Something you stay up late to finish on Thursday night, up to your neck in a hot bubble bath so that you can pass it to your buddy at lunchtime on Friday for her to read over the weekend. I hope that in some small way, my words give life to your thoughts and inspire you to treat yourself with loving kindness and be the friend to yourself that you would like to find in the physical world. I have come to like the woman I am and I wish all of you the same. I count my enjoyment of my own friendship as one of my greatest blessings. I make better choices because of it.

These pages speak not only to women but also to men who wonder why they wind up feeling empty when they do the best they can on a consistent basis. That is not a gender specific issue. Both men and women get their hearts broken and put out more effort than they get results back. The tone of this book is that it is written about women. That is only because it's the only gender I know how to be. If you can get your male companion or friend to read it, you may be very surprised by some of his reactions. I hope you have the kind of relationship that allows discussion of what you feel. A relationship that ends at the physical level leaves the heart longing. A good woman wants more.

The Birth of a Good Woman
Chapter 1

One day I looked in the mirror and realized that the particular shade of auburn I had colored my hair could not occur naturally in a woman over forty five. That hurt. I had been a redhead for over twenty years and had the attitude to go with it most of the time. I started noticing recent photographs of myself. Young hair on an older looking woman was disturbing. Probably not to other people, but it was to me. What once made me feel better about myself was now making me uncomfortable. The outsides were not matching the insides, something was wrong with this picture.

I had been ill with the flu and used that as an excuse to get the hairdresser to give me only a haircut at the next appointment. I was not willing to force my aching body to sit in a chair for three hours while I was "on the rack" getting my touchup. I remembered the days when only death would keep me from "recharging", as I affectionately referred to it. Every day I inspected the regrowth. It was intriguing. What did this woman look like? Who was that woman trying to come out despite all my best efforts?

By the next appointment, the hairdresser was offering options. Color it to what we think is the natural color, strip out the red, frost in the gray, etc. She was being kind. She wanted to make this easier for me. Moving on is *never* easy. This was not only my hairdresser, this was a woman who had bonded with me through monthly updates of the dramas of our lives, the choices we had to make as we grew and changed more than our hair. Melissa is like a little sister to me, she has always looked out for my dignity. She monitored my "redness" for years, saving me from embarrassing myself at various times when there wasn't a red intense enough to suit me. I chose to approach this in much the same way as I had done most things in my life. Feet first, all the way, do not spare the horses. I defiantly wore my striped hair for months while it grew. I could tell Melissa approved. I felt myself becoming more real with each passing day.

I became amused at how others reacted to this. Most women would look at my hair while they talked to me, sometimes scratching their own head, as though they were reacting to some sympathetic itch. Men would also talk to my hair, sometimes with a puzzled look on their face. Almost as if they wanted to ask if it hurt. I came to enjoy this audience to the unveiling of a mature woman. I was proud of my courage.

Finally after months of forcing myself to not give in to the habit of covering up who I am, I looked in the mirror to see the most striking silver streak surrounded by the best frosting "job" I had ever seen in my life. My skin, my eyebrows, my eyes, and most importantly, my very soul coordinated perfectly with my hair. Some treated me differently, a little softer, a little gentler. On the other hand, maybe that was me reflecting back to myself through the eyes of others. I read somewhere once, "Life has a way of mirroring truth back to us in its own way and time." That particular saying was one of those things that I could have written but did not, my thoughts captured in another person's words waiting for me to discover them when it was time for me to hear the truth. It is proof of a connection between people who have never met, but have walked the same path. Discovering words that belong to you, written or spoken by another person is one of the miracles in life, in my opinion.

No longer was I an older woman with a hair color not found in nature. The outsides were starting to match the insides. It felt good. The streak was a badge of honor that I wore proudly. The compliments came. I was asked where I got my hair "done". A neighbor's child, standing quietly and obviously staring at my hair while her mother and I chatted in the bright sun, remarked in a very serious tone, "Miss Susan, you gots sparkles in your hair." Yes, I do. I feel so lucky to have sparkles in my hair. Not everyone realizes what an honor it is to wear them well. Sometimes you just know what the right thing to do is. Listen to the message when it comes, you will be glad you did.

SUSAN V. DARDEN

How Do You Get There From Here?
Chapter 2

I don't think any one specific thing caused me to start questioning so many facts about the way my life was going. Let's just say the natives were restless. Nothing was really wrong, yet very little seemed to be going right. There were times that I seemed to be at a standstill. Over time, I came to realize that even nothing was a sign that something was possibly amiss.

Life truly is a journey and not a destination. Nothing stays the same forever. Change is imminent. The human mind tends to view times that are disturbing, painful or inconvenient as permanent and times that are happy and rewarding as temporary. Even the greatest optimists have times of depression and lack of motivation. I have learned that life is like the weather in the Tidewater region of

Virginia, if you don't like it, wait a day or two, it will be totally different again.

I had lived a life of working hard at whatever was in front of me to do and I expected that everything would be the way I was told it would be. I have always been responsible, almost to a fault at times. I would marry, have children, have a house, two cars, a nice lawn, be well respected in the community and retire to putter around the house and pursue the recreational endeavors that I had postponed all my life. I didn't wanna. I still don't wanna. Now I know that I'm not gonna, either.

I wasn't always like that. For many years I moved toward all those very goals. A lot of things didn't turn out the way I thought they would. The business world changed over the twenty-five years I was out in it and so did I. My marriage didn't work out, even though I waited until I had established an identity for myself first and had achieved a lot of goals independently. I loved him, he loved me. It wasn't enough; we let too many things get in the way.

I enjoyed being a homeowner but found out that it was a second job to maintain one properly, not to mention being a constant money drain. Familial obligations on holidays caused problems, each party wanted to spend them with their own family, instead of treating the entire group as one. The individual families wouldn't stand for it, and we allowed one or the other to have their way, until eventually we each went to our own, alone. As a couple, we would have probably rather been somewhere else, time off being such a hot commodity with our dual career, bustling weekday schedules.

I knew I couldn't have children of my own from a very young age. I had always pictured myself as being a mother at some point in my life in spite of that fact. When I married, we talked about adopting but by the time we had been married long enough to be considered a "stable" couple, we weren't a "stable" couple anymore. After my divorce, most men I dated had children from previous relationships. I figured I would recognize my child when I saw him or her. It hasn't happened yet, unless you count *me*, I have learned how to mother myself finally.

All my life I had heard the expression that "life is simple, people complicate it." Life really IS simple. People DO complicate it. I don't know how it is we come to do that. Young children seem so competent at the very skills we older adults have to consciously recultivate. I believe that you lose what you take for granted. I think the first time you walked by a puppy without stopping to play with it, you went downhill. That's just my opinion, but I have seen evidence of the truth in that everywhere I have turned looking for an answer to the "why?" question. We get in such a big hurry to "get there" we miss a lot of the sights along the way.

I took myself way too seriously for way too long. I thought the world judged my insides by my outsides. They probably did and still do sometimes. I just don't care about it as much as I did at one time. All I know is life lived from the inside out instead of the outside in feels much better to me. I have been around long enough to know that bad people sometimes *look* really good and what your heart longs to do is usually *exactly* what you should be doing. The longest days are spent doing things that you really don't want to do. Longer days are spent doing them with someone you don't want to be with.

It doesn't take a lot to make me happy anymore. Meaningful work in an amount sufficient to pay my bills, healthy loved ones, feeling that I make a difference in someone's life, being able to paint my toenails without grunting, allowing myself my individuality in spite of what your idea of success is.

Many things happened in my life to change my way of thinking. The details of the events are not nearly as important as the changes themselves. I don't consider myself substantially unique. In fact, the older I get, the more I see myself in others. We all have unique traits and abilities that make us who we are, but the common thread that I see that weaves us all together is our shared need to be loved and accepted for exactly who we are. My favorite people are those who allow me to be myself. I do my best to extend them the same courtesy. It's a challenge to walk what you talk, but it makes you stronger and firmer in your resolve to do things the way they work best for you.

The greatest lessons have come to me from the simplest events. That's probably true for most people, I just happen to find it amazing. I find it so amazing that I feel the need to share what I have learned with almost anyone who will listen or read about it.

I recently started going to church again. I had only been to church for weddings and funerals since my mother stopped making me go in the sixth grade. I had developed distaste for organized religion, but maintained a very close relationship with the higher understanding I choose to call God. I have always considered myself spiritual rather than religious. I found a church that I liked recently; it has a little "new age" flavor, just like me. I knew I was in the right place when I walked in and saw there were Kleenex boxes under the seats. I live like I mean it, I like being in places that let me do that. I cry less because of it. If you invite someone to your house and expect them to open their heart, have some Kleenex handy. Sometimes life makes your heart leak.

Success to me today is very different than the success I spent so much energy chasing after years ago. Today I point to my nine-year-old SUV with pride and say I will be driving the wheels off it. There was a time that not all the coupons in the first payment book were used up before it was replaced with another one. I no longer find it prestigious to work for a company that requires me to spend almost half my salary to dress the way they expect me to, just to be able to say that I work there.

The man of my dreams doesn't necessarily have an impressive title or huge bank account. He isn't required to be a "looker." He is more likely to know what I like in my coffee and how important it is that he actually participate in my life, rather than just help direct it. I hope to be some special Grandpa's crazy girlfriend one day. He needs to have the energy to look for shells on the early morning beach, and sit on the dunes smelling the hurricane wind with me. In return he will have my undying devotion and my promise of passionate living.

Where there were racks of clothes, some still with tags attached in multiple closets, there is appropriate clothing to live a juicy life. I refuse to work dawn to dusk for someone else to earn money to pay yet another person to do what I love to do for my family and myself. This girl has an electric screwdriver and knows how to use it.

I do not think for a second that just because I have silver in my hair that I am now finished learning. The best is yet to come. I have learned how to listen to the messages, that means there will be even more messages to hear. Lessons are everywhere, everyday. Open your eyes and your heart, the education of a lifetime is all around you.

The Law of Charlie

Chapter 3

When I started dating my ex-husband, Bob, I knew he had a dog. A dog he talked about a lot. After our second date, Bob took me by his house to meet him. Charlie. I knew he was a Dalmatian. I knew Bob loved him and that fact was one of the things I found very appealing about Bob. I had been a "pet person" all of my life and I knew how a fur or feather bearing creature could become a dear friend and even a "child", especially to a person living alone. To meet a man who was comfortable with admitting his attachment to his pet was refreshing and very attractive to me.

Nothing prepared me for the moment Bob opened the door of his house. Little did I know this spotted beast would become one of my teachers in this never-ending school of life.

There stood the most beautiful Dalmatian I had ever seen, larger than most, attractively marked, strong and actually beaming with love and delight. You could feel positive energy radiating from Charlie. The love at first sight that I felt for him was mutual. The chunk of leftover steak from dinner in my purse probably had something to do with that. I became "Momma" immediately. This was my first clue that Bob and I were getting "serious," in fact. Charlie knew my name was "Momma." Anything said about "Susan" was ignored, but one utterance about his "Momma" was met with instant, undivided attention. He was fascinated and attentive to everything I did.

Charlie thought that if you could operate a whipped cream can you were a magical being. He would stand in front of the oven and watch a turkey roast through the glass window with the same concentration that his master used when watching his favorite team play football. I told more than one person that if they ever needed to break into the house, carry a pizza box and wear a red baseball cap. Charlie would find a way to unlock the door. Having his name called repeatedly while he was napping had no effect, but touch an ice cream bowl in the cabinet on the opposite side of the house and he instantly appeared. Charlie always heard only what appealed to him.

If you ever said, "Let's go for a walk," you had better mean it. His large spotted head on your lap, with alternating eyeball rolls and deep sighs would shame even the worst procrastinator. He was convinced that everyone who came to our house was there to see him. He would show his appreciation by gathering all his toys at the feet of the visitor, never taking his eyes off me. Company meant there was a strong possibility of snack foods; if not, there would at least be some fun and camaraderie.

In the weeks and months that followed, Bob's friends would tease him about how he must "miss" his dog. Bob smiled; he did not seem to have a problem sharing Charlie. I think he was relieved not to be the only one to deal with this massive bundle of unconditional love and joy in living. It can be exhausting to have a companion always in overdrive.

After years of having this dog child by my side almost constantly, I knew him very well. If Charlie got in "trouble" for anything, which did happen from time to time, he would retreat to our bedroom, which had a large doggie bed in the corner, putting himself in "time out", in effect. He would generally fall asleep for a short while. When he woke up, he was convinced that his slate was clean. He would join us in the other room, all wags and enthusiasm, as though we had been gone for a while. His sins were never major, usually something like goosing the cat or leaving the yard when he shouldn't have. If I was upset, he would slink quietly from the room, assuming all responsibility for my unhappiness at the first "damn it" that came out of my mouth, whether it had anything to do with him or not. The incredibly pained look on his face when he retreated to his "time out" spot was comically dramatic and you couldn't help but laugh at him when he returned from having cleansed himself in slumber.

Every day is a new beginning, whether you slept for ten minutes or 10 hours or went to sleep crying or stressed or peaceful and serene. When you wake up, it's square one again. No grudges, no residual issues, total and absolute forgiveness of others and most importantly, yourself; joy and delight in the new day, enthusiasm and wonder in the adventures that lie ahead. Remove yourself from the situation that is causing you pain as soon as possible, rest your body and soul, then try it again. Enjoy the simple things, good friends, good food, and a warm bed. Assume you are loved, unless it is proven that you are not. That is the Law of Charlie. I recommend it highly.

Balance

Chapter 4

Balance has always appealed to me. First, I am a Libra. That explains a lot. Libras are into balance. Secondly, I am an accountant by trade. That explains a lot, too. I was the type of little girl that had a Barbie shoe organizer. I like things tidy (although time has loosened that up a bit) and compartmentalized. I have usually felt at my best when my world did not lean too much one way or the other.

I have always been talented at organizing things and other people. When it comes down to me, the first thing that goes in my life when the going gets tough is, you guessed it, balance. Anything not going well for me will turn me into an unruly child with horrible eating habits, no motivation, and spending hours on the computer or in front of the TV. There will be dishes in the sink, a full trashcan, a shower skipped here and there, no makeup; you get the picture. Living alone does not help this tendency. I found that when I was married, I could force myself to do things out of sheer embarrassment. Sometimes a month or more passes without a visitor in my home, so it is now very easy to put things off or allow my life to turn into the land of slugdom, only becoming semi human for trips to a clients' office or a visit to my parents.

After starting to work out of my home in the past year, and billing clients for time spent on their projects, I have been logging what I do each day in a steno book, which I review weekly to prepare their bills. While recovering from a recent breakup I noticed that I was not getting very much done. Correction. I was getting absolutely nothing done, except for what I was accountable to someone else for.

I decided that those who crumble into a pile of motionless drivel need to be treated as you would treat a child. I thought about a chore list. I thought about a checklist of basic functions that needed to be performed each day. I knew I had to make myself accountable and who better than the closet queen of organizational skills. What I came up with turned me around in a way that nothing ever has before. It is simple enough to not be easy to put off. I had to watch for that too, I was not in the state of mind for complicated routines.

I took a piece of notepaper and wrote, "What have you done to make yourself better today?" at the top. This short list was taped where I would see it several times a day:

- Physical
- Spiritual
- Career
- Family
- Friends
- Home

Each evening I review my log of what I have done that day to ensure that at least one thing in each of these areas has been accomplished. I learned that the first few days, the fulfillments were small. "Home" may have consisted of taking out the trash and making the bed (I was seriously depressed, these things were not happening). The "friends" category was to get me out of my isolation mode. A simple email of a link to a book I liked or forwarding a joke was enough to satisfy that requirement. Someone would respond, I would reply, and a cycle was born. What I found was that after about a week of doing this, my progress was amazing. I had acted *as if* I were in balance, and *get out of town* suddenly I *was*. Within two weeks, I needed more than a page a day in my notebook, where I had been using one page for two to three days during the worst of this period of paralysis.

I had been complaining about how hard it was to get more clients. On the days I didn't have paying work to do, I would mail flyers, find out how to get listed on software websites, get samples of trial versions of software to hand out, call people I used to work for and with, just to be able to check off that I did *something* for my career. Anything to check "career" off that stupid list. I am getting calls and inquiries now. It is amazing to me that these people did not know I was right there waiting for them.

Do not be afraid to be your own mother. It is so natural to guide and nurture another person. Somehow, we overlook how much we ourselves need some wise maternal intervention. Everyone loves feeling needed. Seldom do we think about how much we need *ourselves*. All the skills that you have acquired in your life are not just for the care and feeding of other people. Some days you are the one who needs care. Do not make the mistake of waiting for someone else to do it. I am getting more comfortable with the inner dialog I have with myself in front of the refrigerator now. "Maybe some veggies would be good, you didn't eat any yesterday."

When I find myself stuck in neutral now, I do everything I can to advise myself the same way I would a friend I care about. Because I *am* her. It is no longer excusable to feel that no one cares. *I* am here, *I* care. It takes less emotional energy to be accountable for your actions than it does to worry about how badly you are stuck.

I always wanted a child of my own; little did I know it would turn out to be me.

Who Was That Masked Man?
Chapter 5

More than once, I have looked back over an ended relationship and wondered, how could I have chosen so badly again. The person I started out with, the one who charmed me and captivated my attention was so different from the one I cried over at the end. On the other hand, was he? Did I not look closely enough? Was the heat and passion of the moment enough to make me turn down the volume on the inner voice that knows which ones are keepers and which ones are frogs?

I have come to believe that in at least some of the cases; it was the *potential* of the person I loved and not the person himself. A human being does not come in a kit. What stands before you may very well be all he will ever be. That is not in your control, only his. If you truly love that person, what he is will be enough. A good relationship will enhance what was already good in your life; it will not make you whole in its own right. A bad relationship will make what is good in your life less good and what was bad, worse. Say "Goodbye Frog."

If you persist in pursuing a relationship with someone because of who you want him to be instead of who he is, you are involved in a fantasy with an audience, not a relationship at all. The trauma of a situation like this ending is deep. You must mourn the loss of what you thought you had; fight the self-doubt that comes from thinking it was so real when it wasn't; and then realize that now that you know better, it is no longer excusable to do it again. This is a lot of work for a mere fantasy.

We are most comfortable with behaviors we have practiced before. Changing how we do things rattles the emotional cage. It only feels uncomfortable until you do it once, then that is your way and it comes as naturally as the old way did before. If you like controlling things, put that effort into controlling yourself and not someone else. It is a lot less frustrating, there is actually hope for a good result and you will be challenged enough to keep your mind off what is wrong with the rest of the world. The amazing part is how much everyone else "improves" as you go about the business of managing yourself instead of them.

What he tells you about himself may be what he would *like* to be. That happens when we are selling ourselves, it is not necessarily intentional, we just want what we want and we tend to play up the features to get a buyer. His attraction to you might even be that he sees some quality in you that he wishes were part of *his* personality.

The possibilities are endless; there are as many different scenarios as there are different people in the world. No matter how you meet a person or how long you know them, one fact remains; you only know what they *choose* to let you know about them. This comes as a disappointment to the control freaks of the world, I know, but it is very true.

Time spent with any individual is your best hope of getting a true picture of how they really are. Until you have seen someone sick, stressed, disappointed and angry, chances are there is a part of their personality you are not familiar with. In the intense moments of new attraction, hasty decisions are sometimes made involving life changing situations. Slow down. Time answers all questions. The whole situation does not need to be sorted out and permanent decisions made today. Real love will wait for the timing to be right for both of you. Every person who enters your life for however long they stay serves some purpose, even if it is only to show you what you *do not* want. The timing is right when issues are not being forced. It will flow, like your feelings and not get bogged down in the quagmire of your thoughts.

No one ever taught me how to say goodbye to the frogs. I developed the habit of digging in and trying to make a situation work, even those that had so very obviously taken a hard left and veered off into the ditch. There was a time in my life that I walked away quickly at the first sign of something not being right, I started to feel that I was giving up too soon, and not being fair. I am a person of each extreme before I settle somewhere in the middle. Listen to that inner voice. Tell your head to stop with the "yes buts" for just a minute. What you hear in your gut is what you should listen to when it comes to your feelings. Feelings that travel to your head for analysis will be polluted by learned behaviors every single time. What works in theory does not always match reality. Your inner voice has the ability to see past the mental mumbo jumbo and address the heart (no pun intended) of the matter.

A trusted advisor explained a simple system to me recently that I am trying for myself. He said that when you desire a new relationship to come into your life, you should list at least 10 key qualities that this person should have to be attractive to you. List the ones important to *you*, not the ones you *think* should be there. If the person you are interested in has seven or more of those qualities, proceed with your time together and getting to know this person. If they have six or fewer of those qualities, say "Goodbye Frog." Your frog may be the prince someone else is looking for. Do not waste his time or yours. The sheer exercise of making this list will help you to focus on what you want out of a relationship and will send your intentions out to the Universe, instead of the fears of what could go wrong in one, and the ghosts of what has gone wrong in the past. Focus on what you *do* want to avoid attracting what you *do not* want.

In making my 10-point list of desired qualities, I made a startling discovery. These were all traits that I was seeking to perfect or acquire for myself. In order to find the right person, you have to *be* the right person. When you *are* the right person, you won't have far to look. This does not mean that you are looking for an opposite sex clone of yourself, but it does prove that good relationships need a foundation of shared priorities and fundamental beliefs. Like attracts like, don't become what you fear most, only to attract yet another frog. If you are spending time with a frog, you will be too distracted to see the prince ride up.

Life is meant to be shared with a loving partner. There are enough projects in the world to satisfy your need to create. A person should not be a project; they should be a complete person *before* you invite them into your life. You should be complete before you accept his invitation to enter *his* life. To merge forces before the time is right for both is an open invitation for even the best potential match to fall in ruins.

If you find yourself trying to change him for the sake of your own happiness, do him a favor and let him go to the one who finds him imperfectly perfect for her. Both of you will be spared immeasurable heartache and frustration. If who he is does not meet your needs today, he will not meet your needs tomorrow either unless he chooses to adapt himself. If either of you changes beyond what you want for yourself, the respect of the other partner will eventually be lost and the relationship would end anyway.

Let your union with another person flow into your life through its own power, not yours; and soothe you, not place additional demands on your energy. Any relationship that makes your shortcomings larger and your strong suits weaker has a frog in it somewhere.

SUSAN V. DARDEN

Hunger

Chapter 6

I am fortunate that I have never known what it is like to be without enough food to sustain life. There have been times in my life that I wished there was some way I could live without eating again, however. Having none at all sometimes seems that it would be better than battling something as seemingly harmless in its own right as food is.

People who have trouble stopping their drinking after a couple of beers, can't have just a partial pack of cigarettes around, or who will snort the whole bag of cocaine instead of just getting a party buzz, can stay away from the source of their temptation, giving them a bit of a leg up on abstinence. I do not in any way diminish the commitment those addicted to these substances must show to refrain from indulging in their drug of choice. The person who chooses to fill the nagging void in their soul with food cannot totally abstain. The club they beat themselves with must be faced head on several times a day.

Someone who drinks a little too much or gets high on the weekends can *usually* keep that fact secret from the world if they choose. The food medicaters do not get that luxury. The pounds pile on. Not enough to be morbidly obese in most cases, just enough to keep right on feeling bad about themselves. More ammunition for the already battered self-esteem that starts the destructive cycle. Their pain and lack of self-control is worn for the world to see…the fat suit. The shame can and often does lead to more of the same behavior.

Society in general can be very cruel when it comes to this issue. Many people believe that willpower alone can make a change in this behavior. Part of the recovery process in dealing with a food addiction is learning that just because someone else says something does not make it a fact. Your truth lies within you, not them. Few of these individuals realize that food-addicted people are harder on themselves emotionally than anyone else ever could be. Fewer still, understand that the person in the fat suit has an enemy that can only be controlled by constant, self-loving awareness.

There are those who eat too much just because they like to. Food tastes good. It gives sensory pleasure through smell, texture, taste and sight. I envy those people. Food is all those things to me but with the added twist of making my emptiness temporarily full. I have developed skills over the years that have helped me deal with this tendency, but I believe that once a person eats compulsively for reasons other than hunger, they never completely get over it. It is always there, like a loaded gun. It can have the same effect too, wounding a spirit already battered by feelings of failure and lack of control.

I am fortunate in that I have become able to recognize what is hunger, what is appetite and what is medicating behavior. It has taken years to learn these differences in my own life. I can measure my emotional and spiritual health by the number on the scale. When I feel that I don't somehow meet my own expectations in a situation, one of the first things I want is something to eat. In my case that would preferably be something creamy, cool, and sweet. Everyone is slightly different. If you indulge in this type of behavior, awareness is your best friend. Pay attention to what you do and when. I can often "talk" myself out of medicating myself with food. Sometimes I don't quite make it there in time. It's not a perfect world. I have forgiven many people for a lot of things in my life; it's time to forgive *me* now. I believe that as long as I respect the power I have given this behavior in my life, I will be able to cope with it. Beating myself up over it only makes it worse. Death by Twinkies, only some of you will understand what a true danger that really is. Emotional death is as real as the physical.

I have lost enough weight in my life to build another woman or two. I have never reached my top weight again, for that, I am grateful. I will never forget how sad it made me to see one particular photograph of me in my early twenties. I knew that young woman was not the real me, but didn't have the skills at that time to help her get out of the fat suit. In some ways, the fat suit has served me well.

It goes on when I feel vulnerable and unfulfilled. It protects me when I don't feel capable of handling one more superficial rejection, real or imagined. It is "unzipped from the inside" (thank you Dr. Phil) when I have the self-esteem, emotional and spiritual health to trust that I can handle my own feelings and be responsible for them. The fat suit has been worn for too many years and it is time to leave it behind for the last time. The size of the suit may not shrink to meet society's standards, but once it allows freedom of movement and loss of inhibition, it is just the right size for the wearer.

Diets only work for the people who eat because it tastes good. For the rest of us, I would like to point out that the first three letters spell "die." It is another way to die a slow, frustrating, emotional death from the tortures of negative self-talk. Another way to prove to yourself how you have failed the first time you eat a bag of cookies because you weren't high enough on the "perfect" scale that day. Draw on your internal parent to combat this; no one knows more about food than a compulsive overeater does, the last thing you need is a lecture on calories or fat grams. The answer does not lie in depriving yourself of nourishment. You were not bad and now should be deprived of food in punishment. Get honest, be real about this. *It is not about what you eat, it's what is eating you.* Prepare your meals as though you are serving it to someone you love, someone whose health is of the utmost concern to you, then *you* eat it. This will get you through a difficult time until you can do it because it is good for you and not just what you *should* do. Act as if food is for your nourishment, not your destruction and it will become so. Focus on providing the nutrition to fuel the machine destined to do your life's work. Emotional and spiritual hunger has to be fed with emotional and spiritual food. If you want cake, bread is never satisfying. You can eat a truckload of it and still long for cake. Have a piece of cake when you want it, just take responsibility for what you are doing and stop blaming your weight on other things.

The first time I dieted myself down to a normal weight; it was like visiting a foreign country. I could buy clothes without anguishing over whether they were size appropriate. Both men and women treated me very differently. My mother couldn't stop trying to feed me, I think it made her very uncomfortable to suddenly have a thin person as a daughter. Change was never easy for her either. I focused more on a superficial world than on my emotional growth. I had my heart broken a few times because of it. I gained my weight back.

The second time I dieted myself down to a normal weight, I had already seen the tour book, so I did a little better. I enjoyed the attention, the acceptance in public, my pretty clothes, the feeling of control I had over my body. I married a frog, or the man I married married a frog, I don't remember which way that went now. I focused more on my husband's wants, house and obligations than on my spiritual self and my own needs. My mother couldn't stand how unhappy I was so she baked me a little something. It didn't even take the edge off the longing for a "full" feeling. I gained my weight back.

The third time I dieted myself down to a normal weight, I had had a revelation. My life was out of control. Something had to change;

the pain of staying the same was unbearable. I was involved in a whole house renovation that had run amuck, my husband was having an affair with his assistant, I had changed myself so much in an attempt to make it all work out that I no longer recognized myself. I walked hundreds of miles in the dark with Charlie talking to the stars about how there was no gravity the earth just sucked and reminding him that light posts, not mailboxes were allowable rest stops. My way of coping with the runaway train of my life was to control my weight. A small part of me believed that if I were beautiful, everything would be ok. Those were the days that I believed only thin women could be beautiful. Nothing was ok. I left Bob (and regrettably, Charlie). The guilt, sense of failure and grief of walking away from a whole life I had worked very hard to build opened the hole in my world again. I was very, very empty. I gained my weight back.

Enough of this punishing myself for what are the ups and downs of life; at some point in my journey, I took on responsibilities and perceived powers that were never mine. Blaming myself for failing or not measuring up to what was never in my control to begin with made me incredibly *hungry*. Not for food, though. The menu for a hungry heart lists forgiveness, acceptance, peace of mind, openness of spirit and willingness to change what is not working, instead of blindly hitting the wall repeatedly.

This time I am going to live instead of die again. I am beautiful right now, even in a fat suit. I am whole, complete and a perfect me. I am a good woman. This time will be different. It will be different because I am different. If not one more pound comes off this soft body of mine, I will still be ok. My stretch marks are the battle scars of a war with myself. Until you accept who and what you are, the chances of a lasting change are slim (I find it interesting that I could not find a different word that fit there).

Today I feed my soul a balanced diet of love, acceptance, intellectual and spiritual stimulation. Be sure to supplement your meal plan with those things to completely satisfy your hunger. After you eat, be sure and enjoy some humor as your dessert. It ensures that you remain playful and takes the edge off what can easily look like deprivation instead of self-improvement. Try not to play with "frogs," they are fun for a while but leave you feeling empty. I look at my plate to see if I would wish this meal on a friend, it's the only way I can be sure that I am treating myself with the love and respect I deserve.

I lost three pounds last week. Last night I felt like I wanted to eat New Jersey, but I didn't. I don't have to anymore. The hole is filled with a life that is uniquely, beautifully mine. It doesn't have to work for anyone else. I am a perfect me. It's getting easier to be a good woman every day.

SUSAN V. DARDEN

Never Wear Shoes That Hurt
Chapter 7

In my younger days, I was a shoe freak. During one of the times that I had stepped out of the fat suit, someone admired my legs. In hindsight, I think it was a podiatrist or chiropractor concerned about his retirement. Within months, I owned many pairs of four-inch spike heeled stilettos. I wore them almost 12 hours a day, 5 days a week and usually several hours on Friday and Saturday nights. They looked great, but hurt after an hour or two. I should have stopped immediately. Pain means that something is wrong. Listening to that is a very good idea.

Anything that you do for an extended period of time that goes against the natural order of things causes distortion. There is usually discomfort while it is going on. If that discomfort is ignored, there will be consequences. Deal with it now or deal with it later.

Eventually your feet will not tolerate the wrong shoes. I have decided that wearing shoes that hurt, living with "love" that doesn't love back, doing meaningless work for not enough money, or even earning enough money only to feel restricted and stuffed into a role that isn't me is simply not worth the price that I pay in the long run.

Choices you make to satisfy others ideas of what you should be never bring the satisfaction you thought that they would. Maybe to *them* temporarily, but not to you. Pleasing someone else by doing or trying to be something against your nature will never make you happy. If you do it long enough you will have to learn how to be yourself again should you ever choose to stop it. Feet struggle to adapt to shoes that don't fit. They never quite make it. The other person will sense that you are not real and will seek their quality relationships elsewhere. The same way your toes prefer warm sand instead of pointed shoes. It just feels better. If it hurts, stop it immediately.

I am the first to admit that I am sometimes too independent for my own good. I don't ask anyone to share that responsibility with me. I am a divorced woman with a new, very small home based accounting business, not much in the way of savings, with a passion for being understood (mainly by me but I like it when others "get it" too). I have been known to make major changes in my life because what I was doing wasn't working. Eventually I am going to get it right. I will know by how I feel, not by what I think.

I quit a very good job last year, one that paid decent money and had benefits, because it didn't "fit." Never once have I been afraid that I made a bad choice. I almost felt that I owed it to those who can't choose that path because their choices affect other people. For those who always wanted to free themselves from conventional ways of earning a living and living their life but couldn't, I have taken off my shoes. The hardest part about it has been accepting how others have reacted to my choice. The amazement in their faces when I gave up my "security" for the unknown made me realize that I was glad I knew what "security" really is.

Security, like most truly valuable attributes, comes from inside of you not outside. It is a feeling not a possession, it cannot be taken away from you without your permission. If you base your worth on someone else's provision of a life for you, you have given them your security. Security is knowing that no matter what situation you find yourself in, you can take care of it. Security is competence as a human being. I can do that. When I left my last job, I was asked if I had another one. The answer was "yes I do." I take care of me full time. I trust in my ability to face whatever I need to face to live a life that doesn't hurt. I will have a full time job for the rest of my life. I feel very secure.

The only thing certain in life is change. Change doesn't scare me anymore. Taking off the shoes that aren't quite right for you makes you feel better and there's always another pair just waiting for you to find them and take them home with you. Just remember, you have to go get them, they don't come looking for you.

I have survived the ending of a marriage that I thought would last forever, being laid off from a job I thought I would retire from and what I thought was the love of my life just stopping our relationship with no explanation after a year of promises and plans, along with other assorted trials and tribulations over the years. I won't say that I welcomed these changes into my life at the time. They all hurt. I kicked, I screamed, I cried. They all sat me down in shock on the dusty road of life. I got up eventually. It gets very boring watching the backs of other peoples heads all the time. The world stops for no one. I see now that as those doors closed, others opened. Not necessarily the ones that I would have chosen to open, but ones I was meant to walk through. If your feet hurt, you don't notice the scenery as you proceed on your journey. What you see as you walk the path is important. You don't want to be looking down all the time.

The more things that come into your life and then go away for some reason, the more you realize how replaceable they all are. There will always be another job, another car, another house, another frog, another pair of shoes. Change what you can if it hurts not to. Have yourself a good cry to cleanse the old hurt and embrace the changes you didn't ask for but got anyway. They will only be strangers to you for a short while. Negative energy of any kind burns more daylight than positive. You need your energy to move forward. Wiggle your toes in the warm sand. Don't forget to tie your shoes when you finally put them back on. You will trip sometimes anyway, but there's no sense in asking for trouble.

Do something that you love. You know you love what you are doing by the quality of your end result. No one needs to say that it's good, you just know that it is. In my case, I catch myself wondering how I ever had time to work for someone else. My clients, my writing and my own blossoming life keep me extremely busy. I would have probably had more money in the bank in the short term had I kept my job, but I would have been the same year older and limping from shoes that didn't fit. I feel more secure now than I ever have in my life. A person whose job it is to take good care of themself can always earn a buck when needed.

I look very cute in dorky shoes and I can walk a lot faster, too.

SUSAN V. DARDEN

Who Bought This Dress?
Chapter 8

I have two walk-in closets full of clothes and very little to wear. I have felt at times that someone else stores her clothes in my apartment. I wish she would fork over some rent money. The home improvement and personal organization theme shows on TV recommend that you dump out the contents and only put back what you have used in the past year. The thought of that makes my jaw drop. I would admire anyone who can do it without looking back.

My approach has been gentler. Improvement does not have to mean drastic change all at once. One bag a month goes to charity. I consider it a bill and that seems to make it happen on time. I take my obligations very seriously so I feel guilty if I don't do it. Anything that would possibly work for someone I know goes directly to them, anything else goes in the charity bag. I am seeing slow, steady improvement and experiencing fewer time delays when getting dressed. Sometimes I can even actually find what I am looking for in there. I often find things I didn't even know I had but can now use. I consider those finds to be bonus rewards for a job well done.

The clothes are more than just clothes to me. They represent money I have spent and time that I took to distract myself by shopping instead of addressing what was wrong at the time. I am not in a position financially these days to replace them all. That's not intended to be an excuse, since I don't need that many clothes. No one needs that many clothes. I don't wear them, but it's part of that false sense of security we all get from tangible things. Emotional baggage on hangers. A three dimensional scrapbook. It proves to me that I am still learning that security comes from inside of me, not outside. Two walk-in closets full of clothes that are paid for symbolized success for me so long that now I have to retrain myself. What I paid for them is now beside the point, what they are costing me in time, distraction and storage issues is the focus.

An elderly relative said to me once, "If you don't get rid of things as they become useless to you, eventually your things own *you*, instead of you owning your things." Clothes have owned me. How sad is that? I have heard her words in my head so many times the past few years. I never liked that woman, she made sure I didn't have reason to, but by golly, she had a point there. I strive to live her message on a daily basis. I do not want to be "owned" by anything. I resent even thinking about that concept. Lots of closet space has always been a key selling point to me as far as a place to live is concerned, so I can clearly see how it has already influenced my decision-making. I have chosen closets over a view or something more beneficial more than once in the past.

I moved my clothes to the attic when we remodeled our house when I was married. I moved them back downstairs into closets designed to hold much more than any one person could ever wear. I moved them to an apartment when I got divorced. I have moved them again since then. Some fit in size, some don't. In some cases, even if they fit in size, I am not the same woman who bought them. If they suddenly fit tomorrow, I wouldn't wear them. They are the ones making it to the "monthly" bag first. The "who bought this dress?" cut. I have given myself one year to get into the ones that fit *who* I am but not the size that I am. That will be the "she was smaller (or bigger) than I am" cut. At some point, you have to accept yourself the same way you accept others. It is what it is, time to move on.

There is a dress in there that was an omen to my doomed marriage. Ordered from some obscure catalog in the Southwest, I was sure no one at his new company would be wearing anything like it, considering that we were on the Midatlantic coast. It was a two pieced, elegant dinner suit in forest green, unusual in design and color. When we arrived at the party, his assistant was wearing the same dress. Three years later, her affair with my husband would finish off an already wounded relationship. There are no coincidences in life. I have kept the suit for a while to remind myself to pay attention to the nuances of life, they fairly scream at us sometimes. That one sure did.

The wedding dress that I bought more for my mother than for me is in there, too. She wanted a wedding for her only daughter. I was anything but Scarlet O'Hara. The dress looked like what Scarlett would have worn. I swore that I would never wear anything with a bow on the bum. It had a very big bow on the bum. Never say never.

I keep my donation bag next to the dryer in the laundry room. Anything that felt funny, wasn't comfortable, or made me self-conscious last time I wore it goes in the bag as soon as it is washed, along with the shoes that hurt the last time I wore them. I am hoping to move again in the next year or so, I refuse to carry someone else's clothes up and down flights of stairs again. The ones that are really mine are heavy enough.

When I was in my late teens, I spent a lot of time with my great aunt. She was a grandmother figure in my life. She was a very overweight woman and had trouble navigating her steep attic stairway and crowded little house. Her house had tiny closets. Even though she only went out once or twice a week they were stuffed with similar styled dresses (muumuus, actually) of very bright colors, predominantly red or some large print with red in it. She wore the same three or four over and over. Twice a year I would go to her house and rotate the dresses from the closets to the attic, side stepping all the shoes that hurt which were parked on the attic stairs from top to bottom, bringing the winter muumuus down, taking the summer muumuus up; reversing that process every six months. I swore I would never do that. Never say never. It was a rehearsal of what was to come for me. What you don't learn on your first trip through an experience, you can pick up on your way back around. Try not to repeat the same lesson too often, there is much more to learn once you see yourself clear of each exercise.

Newer houses come with bigger and bigger closets all the time. Do we need more clothes now than the women decades ago? If you look at houses built in the fifties and sixties the closets are very small by comparison. If I take what I actually wear, what I feel good wearing, and what fits my lifestyle; put it in one section of my closet, it is roughly the same amount of space as closets I have seen that I called "too small." *Having* more doesn't make *you* more. Having what you need makes you feel competent, however. It at least keeps you from spending excessive energy on mere clothing. It should not be an issue, get dressed and go live.

If I could relive my life just knowing what I know now about clothes, I could save myself a small fortune and a lot of energy. We learn as we live if we pay attention at all. Sometimes no matter what you paid for something, it wasn't a bargain. So many things in those closets were bought for a "feel good." It felt good to have something new, something pretty, something different to give me a "fresh" look. That never lasts. A good feeling cannot be bought; it comes from being well dressed on the inside. A fresh look comes from a centered, confident personality and enthusiasm for your own life. Cloth on a hanger covers your body, that's all; there is no magic there. The magic is in what fills the cloth out.

I have noticed lately that the women I admire most style wise, are the most simply dressed. Their clothes are usually understated and appropriate. The perfect little black dress. The crisp white shirt and well fitting jeans. A beautiful pin or unusual earrings. These are the women who are usually striking, confident, memorable and easy to be around. They have more on their minds than trends and quantity. They have substance and integrity. Good women know what works, they leave the rest behind.

The Gift That Keeps On Giving
Chapter 9

I have never understood why it seems to be so difficult for some people to share what they know in a work setting. I hate to generalize, but it seems that particularly women have a hard time passing on what they have learned through their own experience or education. I have found that this is usually not a conscious withholding of information, but rather some possessive, unconsciously territorial attitude born of insecurity. The same women who withhold information often complain about the male world trying to keep them "down." I have never seen a man keep a woman down as long as another woman will. This needs to stop. Let it start with you. I have.

I was fortunate to learn very early in my career, that every time I taught someone something that I knew, the benefit to me was twofold. First, the fact that someone else now knew how to perform this particular function freed me up to do something else and secondly; every time I taught the task, I became better at it myself. Now why would I not want to show someone how to do what I do? I was never once considered less in the environment I was in because I taught someone else how to do something. If anything, status was gained in that setting.

When you show someone how to do something it does not make you *less*, it makes room in your life for you to be *more*. To me it seems that this even satisfies the inner need most of us have to leave some mark on this world. What better way to achieve immortality than to leave behind your methods, skills and example? Imagine if only one third of the people you have taught, teach someone else and one third of those individuals pass on what they have learned. All because of you. It doesn't get better than this, my friends. Imagine the power that could be generated from passing on information to others rather than keeping it to yourself in futile hopes that it will make you irreplaceable.

Does dying with your special devils food cake recipe make you feel irreplaceable? I guarantee someone, somewhere can make one just as tasty. Why not make some young baker beam with delight over compliments they receive, they will think of you every time they bake one for the rest of their life. Whether we are talking about cakes or how to use computer software or mathematical equations or where certain files are kept or accounting methods, it is all the same; give away some knowledge, you will become more.

Positions can be filled but people cannot be replaced. A person who functions as a teacher or mentor to those around them bring more than their abilities and skills to the table, they offer inspiration and motivation. Everyone loves feeling needed and appreciated. When a moment is taken to pass along a piece of information that you have learned to make someone else's task easier or even just for general information, you make that person feel included and important. This is reflected in how they treat not only you, but also their co-workers and customers. The thrill of seeing this person walk just a bit taller over time cannot be bought or included in your paycheck.

I have been in work and social environments where there has been a person or group of people who hoard what they know or how they do something to the point of being comical about it. I call them information misers. They are easily recognized by their tight little facial expressions, closed body language and rapid mood swings when they are observed talking to someone in authority. One can only hope that eventually they find themselves in a situation in which they are excluded the same way that they exclude others, so that they can see for themselves how ridiculous and counterproductive this really is. I have seen these same people maintain that they are "loyal" or even "dedicated." There is nothing loyal about performing a function for someone who has paid you money for it and depriving others in that group of the information or know-how of how to do it when you are not there. That seems like doing the job half way to me. Their "dedication" is only to themselves as they persist in making themselves feel better in the only way they know how, by making others appear to be less. I for one do not want to be the only one who can do something at work. Indispensable people have a hard time getting a vacation or even a long weekend, in some cases.

One of the things I do in my business now is "coach." I cannot describe to anyone how wonderful it feels to see the light go on for someone formerly in the dark. It makes the light go on for me, too; but in a different way. The gift I give to them becomes a gift I give to myself. I walk a bit taller. I feel "more" than I was before. Someone now has something that I gave them. I often think of the person that showed me how to do what I just passed on. No one is born knowing how to do things. Someone, sometime, somewhere showed you how to do what you do. You put your own spin on it to make it yours, but the seed came from someone else.

I believe that what we take for granted, we are destined to lose eventually. Be grateful enough for your skills and abilities to want someone else to experience the joy and satisfaction of being able to do these things too. It will make you more, not less. They will think of you often and about what a good woman you were.

Jewelry

Chapter 10

I have a vivid memory of looping a fluffy white clover blossom around my finger as a little girl, in the bright summer sun; imagining what it would be like to have a ring from a man who adored me. Even at that tender age, the thought brought me a lot of pleasure. Almost forty years later, I realized it was self-defeating to think that a ring could be proof of anything that mattered.

Our society taught generations of women to value themselves by the men in their life and what they give us. Only when we look back do we know that our true worth comes from things that are not *given* to us, but are *taken* by us. Value as a human being is your birthright, it is not an award bestowed upon you. Claim what you already own. It is all that you need to live well.

SUSAN V. DARDEN

The first time I was engaged to be married, I received a beautiful round cut full carat solitaire engagement ring. I was so proud of that ring. It was a larger diamond than most of the women I knew had. That brought some twisted sense of validation to me. I enjoyed the compliments, the admiration of his good taste in jewelry. In my mind, it was tangible proof that I was wanted and valued.

A few months after I got the ring, I had gotten it very dirty working at a seafood concession with my fiancée and I was concerned about how much I had banged it around in the process. I stopped at a local jewelers to get it cleaned and have the prongs inspected. When I asked the jeweler to take a look at and clean my "diamond" his brow wrinkled noticeably. He pulled out his jewelers loop, examined the ring and asked hesitatingly, "Miss, are you are under the impression that this is a *diamond?*" It was one of those "time stood still" moments. Needless to say, a frog was bidden adieu that day.

I don't think that the individual involved ever really "got" the fact that I didn't care about the ring being fake. If he had said "I am going to buy a cubic zirconium as your engagement ring," I would have either said, skip the engagement ring and let's get something nice as a wedding ring or I may have even worn the cubic zirconium. It's hard to say for sure, I never got the chance to be included in that decision. The cost of the ring didn't matter. What mattered was how being deceived felt. All I really wanted was for him to love me.

Looking back on the experience, I processed that whole situation as not being the frog's fault for deceiving me but rather as some *unworthiness* in me. For years, that memory was in the filing cabinet of my subconscious, proof positive, in my thinking, that I was unlovable and somehow not doing something right. Now I realize how very sad the whole thing was from his standpoint. He felt that he had to deceive me to have me be his wife. I hope he has forgiven himself.

The man I eventually married was the opposite extreme. He took me along to the lapidary to select the stones for the ring that would be made just for me. He would only consider "investment grade" stones. I never quite understood all that. I couldn't picture myself selling an engagement ring for profit at any point in my life. Quite a production was made of this whole process and we wound up selecting a near carat flawless marquis stone for an engagement ring.

I had to give this ring up about a week before the wedding for the band to be changed and two large trilliant cut sapphires to be nestled up against the marquis. My fiancée and I had decided that one ring suited us better, and with his insistence that all the stones be "investment grade", he would not be able to afford much more at that time.

The ring was so valuable that I only wore it when I left the house. As soon as I came in, I removed it and placed it in a jewelry box. It was for public viewing and "investment" purposes only. I just wanted him to love me. I was complimented on it almost daily. There was no mistaking that it was very special. My husband would take my hand across the dinner table when we were out, not to hold it or to connect with me, but to admire the ring and what a good "job" he had done. Anyone who remarked that it was lovely in his presence would get the story about how he selected the stones himself and they were "investment grade." I knew all the time that the ring's only value was monetary. It just took awhile to admit it to myself.

After we were married about five years, we had a "wedding" ring made to fit against the original ring. The stones were carefully chosen to match. It took months for the lapidary to obtain the exact shade of matching sapphires to add two more trilliants. I believe the only reason that second ring was made was because a couple of older relatives remarked that I still didn't have a wedding ring. Quite honestly, by the time it was complete, I thought it was rather gaudy even though most who saw it complimented it profusely. It didn't feel as good as the clover blossom ring I dreamed over as a child. Most people would remark that I had a "good husband."

During my marriage, I received several more pieces of "good" jewelry. All "investment grade." When the divorce settlement was done, their value appeared on my side of the property division. They turned out to be my "investment" after all. I would never consider selling any of them. The lessons they brought to me are priceless, I don't ever want to forget them.

The ring I wanted was just like his Aunt Laura's ring. Laura was close to ninety when her husband of almost 50 years passed away. She still called him "Sweetie" until the day he died and referred to him that way after he was gone. Her ring was a thin gold band, dinged and somewhat misshapen after years of gardening, loving a man, living her life. Laura would never have taken her ring off to store it in a jewelry box while at home. They had lived what it stood for, a continuous unbroken circle of love. It would eventually have to be cut off her hand. I want one of those one of these days. Unfortunately, only a lucky few ever get a ring like that, even fewer appreciate it for its true value.

When a woman marries, she usually gets nice jewelry to commemorate the event. While I was going through the divorce process, it occurred to me that divorce was just as life changing and was every bit as big a milestone as marriage. I bought myself a beautiful gold necklace and matching bracelet. It was very healing. I call it "the divorce necklace" to this day. I wear the set several times a week. I feel very good when I wear it; it was a gift from someone who loves me a lot. A long overdue expression of sincere commitment.

The little girl with the clover blossom ring had the right idea after all. Life comes full circle and our youngest, purest thoughts often turn out to be the right ones. What the jewelry is made of doesn't matter. The joy that a clover blossom ring or a buttercup necklace brings reaches farther and lasts longer than the most precious of gems if crafted in love and with pure motives. The best jewelry comes from the heart, and lasts forever even if only in your memory.

SUSAN V. DARDEN

Forgiveness
Chapter 11

I have come to believe that forgiveness is the most powerful act in the world. It is the greatest gift you can give to yourself. It is the only thing that can free up a broken spirit to walk the perilous paths of life again after spending time sitting on their rear in the middle of the road; motionless, stunned, afraid and lost. As long as you sit in the middle of the road with your head in your hands, it will hurt, you will feel lost and you will look stunned.

Hurting stops when you let it stop. Forgiveness takes the suffering out of growing pains. *Pain is mandatory in life, suffering is optional.* I am convinced that if it were not for pain, few of us mere mortals would be motivated to do anything to move forward. That is why they are called "growing pains." When the pain of standing still becomes unbearable or simply boring after a while, stop it. Notice how good it feels. I bet you just forgave someone, even if it was yourself.

I have been told that I am too "easy," that I have doormat potential sometimes. I do not believe that forgiving means forgetting. When you forget a lesson that you have learned, and you repeat the action again; or you make excuses for someone's inexcusable behavior, that is being a doormat. I have scraped the "welcome" sign off my forehead. I have indeed been a doormat before, I forgive myself for that. First, I forgave the one who walked on me, discovered that wasn't enough, and then extended myself the same courtesy. Anything less brings me back to the original problem instead of forward to resolution. Another person will only respect you to the extent that you respect yourself. Forgive yourself for disrespecting you. You don't have to do it again if you don't want to.

Two of the heaviest loads you can carry on your journey through life are resentment and anger. As I get older, I find that I cannot carry the loads of my youth; the weight is just too much for me. I have learned that taking a left when hitting a wall is preferable to breaking through it. The only thing I can control is my own behavior. I do not want what I have to force to come into my life; I believe that what is meant to be will come when I am supposed to have it as long as I persistently work toward that goal with good intentions. What is not meant to be will either never come to me at all, or if I force it into my life, it will not stay. I have learned that faith is believing beyond a shadow of a doubt in something you cannot see, but you know it is there all the same and it is for your ultimate good and the ultimate good of everything and everyone you encounter.

Forgiveness is partly about finally acknowledging that not everything is all about you. It is about your soul growing up, no matter what your chronological age. It is stepping out of the self-centeredness of your pain and reaching for more than a band-aid to cover your latest booboo. It is owning the facts and the lessons derived from the situation and moving on to become a more informed, competent human being. There are few things we enter into in this life alone. Have compassion for your partner in that painful lesson. You don't have to let them do it again. You just need to forgive them. So that *you* can go on.

When a heart is broken, usually at least two individuals were present. No one starts a relationship thinking that it will end in hurt and disillusionment. Two people wind up disappointed. No one wins. It is very easy to see only your side of the situation. Truth has two extremes, his and hers. What really happened lies somewhere in the middle. At some point, it has to stop being about the "he saids" and "she dids" and has to start being about the forward movement of life. If it is not working for you, get something that is. Open your heart enough to see more than just your shadow and the ghosts of your pain.

I am the first to admit that forgiveness in all its greatness and value is not an easy thing to do. My early attempts at forgiveness often start out as curses, as in "I hope that bastard gets what he deserves." I am human. It is a process that is necessary to healing.

Gradually it becomes the healthier "I hope he gets all that I want for myself." This can take days, weeks, or months. There are acts that I have forgiven or am working on forgiving that are *years* old. Deal with it now or deal with it later. Like dust on top of the refrigerator, it will be there as long as it takes you to clean it up. It will not "walk" off without your intervention. The emotional burden we place on ourselves by suffering over deeds, thoughts and feelings become heavy enough to eventually do something about them. The alternative is to die a slow spiritual death. It hurts when you do that. Please stop. The sooner the better.

There will be times when you vacillate back and forth. "I take it back, I was right the first time, he is a bastard." Forgive yourself for choosing a bastard; you will progress again when you are ready. Do not think that because you take a step backwards you have failed to forgive. Life is a journey, not a destination. Sometimes you have to look at something more than once to absorb what it means to you. Eventually you will have it memorized; only you know when that is.

The other person hurts, too. At first that made me feel better for the wrong reason. Now it makes me hope that he has forgiven not only me, but most of all, himself. Forgiveness brings your compassion back. Compassion feels much better in your heart than anger and resentment. Nothing happens by mistake, the lessons you learned together potentially will lead you both on to greater good if you let them. This person was your traveling companion; he saw the same sights that you saw. Wish for him the same resolution and peace that you wish for yourself.

Anytime you leave behind something that doesn't serve you well, it makes a space for something that can. Sometimes I start the process of forgiveness by asking for the anger and resentment to be removed. Hint: it helps if you mean it. Once you mean it, it will be gone. Sometimes, you have to mentally manipulate anger and resentment a bit before you are ready to let it go. Enjoy. Wear it out. Have a few revenge fantasies while you are at it, you may get your sense of humor back as a side benefit.

Be sure to say "thank you." I have found that I have truly forgiven when I can say "thank you for the lesson." What we take for granted we often lose. Be grateful often. You never have to do what hurt you again if you don't want to. It's your choice.

If you can't decide whether you want to forgive someone or not, move on to something else. If the topic comes back up in your conscious thought or you find yourself repeating the same behaviors with a different partner or in a different situation or you just can't seem to move forward, consider trying to forgive again. It is worth the effort. We often put more effort into making money than we do into earning self-respect. Take this job on for yourself, the benefits are incredible.

The best part about the effort of true forgiveness is the more you do it, the more room becomes open in your heart for what will never *need* forgiving. I believe that no one can hurt you without getting some pain on themselves. That means that I also believe that forgiving often and thoroughly means that I will be forgiven, too.

SUSAN V. DARDEN

The Wraparound
Chapter 12

We all have our pet peeves. Mine is the little piece or pieces of hair that almost bald men wrap around their head or comb over the bald spot. I try not to look when I see someone that does that. Nevertheless, I do. It distracts me terribly. My mind wanders, I cannot concentrate on what that person may be saying or doing. I find myself in a conversation with myself, saying, "Does he not think we see that he is bald?"

I have to give credit where credit is due though. I think the "wraparound" is one of the things that threw me over the edge with the whole hair color thing. Everyone ages. Everyone has a unique look, style, personality. Some of that comes from who you are on the inside. Some of it comes from genetics, gravity, how hard you lived the first part of your life, environment, and any number of factors. If a wraparound bothers me, I can only imagine what a stark white stripe peaking though intensely red hair can do to someone's concentration when they are talking to me. Not that I ever dared leave the house with it showing until I made the decision to "come out" once and for all. For years, my hair appointment had a place of great reverence on my calendar each month.

To me, a sexy, confident person hides very little. Openness and acceptance in a person's attitude unconsciously makes me feel safe in their presence. If you are open, accepting and honest with yourself, it only makes sense that you will be that way with me. I can concentrate on who I am and my relationship with the other person, with an individual like that and not spend as much time looking for the "gotcha." Does that mean that men with wraparounds are not open, honest and accepting? No. What it means is, my reality is my perception of a situation. I can't help it. If you try to hide the fact that you are bald from me, what else would you be afraid for me to know? I am no longer satisfied with superficial relationships; I want to see who I am dealing with up close and personal, otherwise why bother. The time for game playing has passed for me. This thought process is not a conscious thing, but it happens nonetheless. The reverse is also true, if the person I am in a relationship with is not self-conscious about their body; I am apt to be freer and not want to hide myself either. We give each other permission to be real. Anything less than real is withholding from our partner. Who wants a partner who holds back on *any* level?

LIFE AFTER HAIR COLOR

    I cannot envision myself in an intimate embrace with a man with a wraparound without my eyes wandering to his head. My fingers itch just thinking about it. My hands would long to separate the wayward strand from its unnatural placement, and trim it to match the rest of the haircut so that I can talk to this person in peace. A full head of hair is not on my 10-point checklist of things I desire in a partner. Honesty, self-acceptance and strength of character, are, however. I find those qualities much more attractive than hair.

    I have dated bald or balding men. One had a ponytail but was totally bald on top. That didn't bother me. His wearing a hat everywhere except to bed did sometimes. I have to admit the hat suited his personality and added a lot to his general appearance. However, sitting next to him in front of the fire, sipping our drinks and enjoying the moment hatless didn't leave me not attracted to him. If anything, I was more relaxed and certainly every bit as attracted. I don't think I just imagined that our interactions during those times were of a higher quality. It was a great compliment to be in that man's presence without his hat, he didn't let just anyone see him that way. It looked like he was going to stay a bit instead of rush right out the door. He didn't stay, but that's beside the point.

    Another man that I dated wore a really bad toupee. It's difficult for a man to wear a toupee and have it look natural. I wish they wouldn't try. I enjoyed this man's company and had a lot of fun dating him, but quite honestly I never took him very seriously. Even after we had progressed to sleepovers, he never acknowledged that his hair was not real. Not even the morning he woke up with it turned around backwards on his head and obviously knew that I saw it. He was amazingly fast at turning that thing around but not before I got a quick look. I was proud of the fact that I never forced the issue, it must have been a big deal to keep that information (or think he was) from someone he was that intimate with. Sometimes having a poker face no matter what is going on is the greatest gift you can give someone. No one should have to disclose anything until they are ready. Denial is not something I want to build a relationship around, though.

If people are comfortable with themselves, it takes a lot of the pressure off the other party. If you accept you, chances are you can accept me. I like that. It makes it easier to keep being eccentric when I don't feel that I am making someone uncomfortable with it. That fact frees me up to concentrate on the relationship opportunity in front of me. The person who is accepting and open has a real chance of getting to know me. I never felt right without makeup in front of Mr. Toupee, and bed head was definitely out of the question with him. That was a shame, since I have some of my most brilliant moments with bed head. He never found out about that, I was always too inhibited to let him see it.

In trying to understand the wraparound, I found myself thinking about the things women do to "hide" their imperfections. We do a lot more than just wrap. The female equivalent of the wraparound, in my opinion, is the drawing on of eyebrows where there are none. I have been taken aback by this more than once. Drawn on eyebrows and vividly pink cheeks on an older woman can make my brain shut down as fast as a wraparound. I cannot fathom why someone would shave, pluck or wax away hair to draw some on. Human beings are fascinating creatures; I cannot help but wonder what someone is thinking about when they do something like that. I think the youthful "alert" look is what is being attempted…it just looks like drawn on eyebrows.

Self-consciousness keeps us from living the life we should be living sometimes. I love reading by the pool. It's very hard for me to do that at my apartment complex. The ratio of young hard bodies to soft middle-aged ones is disproportionate (at least poolside). The dilemma for me is, brown fat doesn't look as fat as white fat, and I really like going without pantyhose in the summer. So I go to the pool anyway. It only hurts for the few minutes it takes me to get to a chair and get settled. Once I get myself settled and realize that the hard bodies are all looking at the other hard bodies (and thinking about how they look to each other) and not at us soft middle-aged folk, I can read my book in peace. It's not all about me. Few people have been known to lose sleep over the size of my thighs. I have once or twice, but that's another chapter.

The more you make yourself do things that are uncomfortable to do, the easier it is to try more. Life keeps getting juicier. If you are waiting for yourself to get thin, young, or beautiful before you deserve to sit in the sun, I have a late breaking bulletin for you. All you have is today. None of us knows what tomorrow will hold. What if my apartment managers shut the pool down tomorrow? I would have paid the same rent as the hard bodies and never used the damn thing. Act as if you like yourself enough to let yourself do what you enjoy and it will be so.

Self-image is a very powerful thing. Very few people are as tough on us as we are on ourselves. I have found that there is only one person who has ever expected me to be perfect. Me. Everyone else seems to think I look fine. Especially when I act like I think I look fine to me. That is happening more often these days.

I have seen pictures of myself taken at various times over the years that have startled me with the realization that I was a very attractive young woman. I remember that at the time the pictures were taken I didn't think so. Most of the time I complained about having my picture taken. I was dissatisfied with the image before the picture was ever developed. It would be very dangerous for me to be allowed to go back to that time with the knowledge I have now. God is no fool, He knows that. That is why there is no "reverse" in progressing through life, middle-aged brains could wreck havoc in a truly young body.

I think it is admirable to be the best you can be both inside and outside. One compliments the other. It's a complete package. Perfection exists only in your mind's eye. Beauty truly is in the eye of the beholder. I look pretty much the same from one day to the next. Some days I smile at the pretty lady in the mirror and some days she gets a frown of disapproval. The days she gets a smile seem to go much better on all levels. The days that a frown reflects back usually mean there is business to be attended to that originates below

LIFE AFTER HAIR COLOR

the surface. Put the eyebrow pencil away, it's not going to help you out in that situation.

There are people all over the world who hold back on living their life the way they want to live it because of some self-imposed rule of appearance or entitlement. You worry less and less about what people think of you the more you realize how seldom they actually do. They can't be worrying about your thighs when they are so concerned about their baldhead. If you don't like something about yourself, change it. If you can't change it, learn to love it or at least accept it. There is no need to put yourself on hold until you pass some test that no one but you knows is being given.

Watch a baby for help on this. Most of us are so polluted with negative self-talk and outside expectations, both perceived and real; we have no clue how to be uninhibited. Babies have no concern about their little Buddha bellies and knee wrinkles as they toddle about their day, full of giggles and curiosity about the world around them. No one has told them yet that abs of steel make you an enviable member of society. They seldom notice what someone is wearing unless it occurs to them that whatever it is would feel really good in their mouth. They don't ask Mom to be sure and get them some closed toe shoes because their feet look weird or a vertically striped diaper to downplay their big butt. Often shoes and diapers are pulled off at the first sight of sunshine and water. They want nothing between them and the experience of life.

I don't advocate that we all rip off our clothes and jump in the water...but in the right company it could have possibilities. Choose your company based on their comfort level with themselves, become more human together. Be a little infantile today, assume you are perfect. You are a perfect you. Accept no imitations of yourself.

The Staff Meeting
Chapter 13

For most of my career, I considered meetings to be a necessary evil. I scheduled them sparingly and referred to them often as "the practical alternative to work." Now that I work and live alone, the only real meetings I attend are with clients for the most part. I have come to understand why they are so important in most cases. The true intention of a meeting is to ensure that when multiple parties are working for a common goal, that they communicate their progress and what is left to do with each other. It's about communication, or should be anyway. Working together, not against each other.

I have noticed that in my own life and from observing friends and family that women fill so many roles in their daily lives that often there is internal conflict between obligations, needs and desires. Things feel out of control sometimes even when they are not. I should be writing but the living room needs to be vacuumed. I need to go see a client but I have to pick up a prescription before the drug store closes. The internal dialog starts. Bickering. Blaming. Whining occasionally. Even without the scheduling complications of a spouse and children, my own life is full of ever changing roles for me to play in order to pull off what I need done in a timely manner. Try being your own secretary and see how hard it is not to have someone to blame for your inefficiencies. We can negative self-talk ourselves into crisis where there is none some days.

I joke quite often (especially when I am a few minutes late) that I am coming from a "staff meeting" and it ran over a bit. My clients chuckle and probably think to themselves that were I not so jovial they would consider locking me out of their businesses for security reasons. It's really only sort of a joke. I actually DO have staff meetings. I think everyone needs to at least once in a while.

I sit down every few days with a pad of paper, a calendar, a really big cup of coffee, and my laptop computer. The first thing I do is look over the last list I made. It's usually pretty scribbled on and crossed out, noted on and snack stained. I assess the old business first, rewriting things that are still pending on a fresh piece of paper under one of several categories that I have found over time work for me. I try to keep items in order of importance, but it's not as critical to do this perfectly as it is to bring some semblance of order to your racing thoughts. Just getting the items in some kind of logical sequence on paper gives a sense of ownership to all the free-floating thoughts and needs and internal squabbling.

Most men seem to have little trouble compartmentalizing their thoughts, keeping personal business separate from career matters, leisure activities separate from networking. Men that I have known well have little trouble stepping from one side of their self to the other. I don't think they have the internal dialog problems that women seem to get wrapped up in. They are sometimes jealous that the voices only talk to us, I believe. This is probably why we have to explain so many things to them that another woman would understand immediately. The voices know the real deal.

Women tend to pool their life into one big category called "I Gotta." That's what I write at the top of the sheet of paper. Underneath there are sections for client matters, writing issues, personal errands, family business, phone calls, whatever. I usually have a small section at the end that is headed "would be nice." That's for when I have a light week and can't remember what it was I wanted to do when I finally had time to do it. This sheet, once updated, will live by my laptop computer and be scratched out and jotted on until the next meeting. I think it is more comforting than necessary, but it works for me so I keep doing it. Do not computerize this list. It needs to be in your handwriting. The computer makes it too easy to copy things over that need to be seriously reconsidered. Writing longhand gives you a moment to ask yourself if you really want this thing on your list. Say "no, I won't be doing that this week" at least once while you are rewriting the things from the last list.

This little exercise in thought housekeeping as I like to refer to it, doesn't just serve as a valuable point of reference for obligations or needs that I have, it also frees up critical short-term memory space for actually making the "I Gottas" happen. Do not turn yourself into a list maniac. One sheet of paper, updated once a week. Anything more becomes obsessive I have found, and therefore, counterproductive.

I use the back of the sheet of paper for thoughts of what I want to write about next or what I need to ask my insurance person on the phone, what to pick up at my clients' office, things that occur to me as I go about my day. Do not throw this piece of paper away until you are satisfied that the information not crossed off is on your new sheet. I can tell you a few things about salvaging last week's list from under the coffee grounds sometime, but you will do it too eventually; everyone has to learn for themselves.

Instead of being frustrated and resentful of the many roles you play in the course of each day, learn to enjoy your own diversity. All those women are your girlfriends, enjoy them. I love that I shop for groceries in between the client visit and the banking. In fact, I try to schedule "show time" to alternate with "no brainers." This seems to cut down on fatigue. One of the things that convinced me to gain more control over my work schedule was the stress level I felt by being constantly "on" for ten to eleven hours straight every day. My staff was very unhappy with that arrangement. I do much better alternating intensity of activity. One me rests or goes on autopilot while another self emerges and does her thing.

There is so much in our daily life that we cannot control. I seldom commit to anything happening on a specific day unless it affects what someone else is doing or if it is for paying work. During busy times be sure to get very stingy about what goes on the list. If it doesn't make your immediate future better or help you to reach a long-term goal, do not write it down. The essential things will get done regardless. If a particular item keeps getting copied over and over from week to week, consider dropping it. It hasn't killed you that its not done by now, the chances of you dying over it are probably slim. My former spouse used to say that if you put most things off long enough they would lose their importance. I remember how that statement infuriated me at the time. Bob lived with Charlie so long his sense of urgency was sometimes underdeveloped, or so I thought at the time. I think it's a very profound observation now. The truly important things manage to get done no matter what, the rollovers probably were way less important or something would have happened to cause them to get accomplished.

The main benefit of a staff meeting with the accountant, consultant, writer, daughter, sister, friend, tenant, housekeeper, laundress, chauffer, buyer, student, neighbor, church member, et al is to ensure that all these women stay centered enough to meet the common goals of one very full life and do not squander their time battling it out with each other. They all need to be heard. Each and every one is an essential team member. And my life is a quiet one! I have no idea how the women who have mom, grandmother, wife, ad infinitum on their staff manage it most days. Maybe a bigger sheet of paper or at least a bigger cup of coffee would help them.

SUSAN V. DARDEN

Let the ladies talk to each other when they need to. It helps to relax for that to happen. I have had to chuckle to myself more than once at what I call "a bathtub revelation." A bathtub revelation is the emergence of an answer out of absolutely nowhere when you are doing something totally unrelated. It is usually something you agonized over at length at one time, but gave up on because you just couldn't remember or think of what it was. You weren't listening at the time, probably because you were talking too much. I named it that because quite often, if I am having trouble balancing an account or remembering something, the answer will come to me while in the bathtub…far away from my notepad and laptop. I have been known to repeat a thought to myself over and over while I get a towel so it will remain in my short-term memory while I get something to write on. Bathtub revelations are usually very high quality thoughts and realizations. It's best to put them on paper as soon as possible lest they are snatched away by some less appreciated detail. The bossy one shut up long enough for someone else to get a word in edgewise, let's try to not interrupt her.

Becoming eccentric is something that I am enjoying. I have always been a little that way, but I am putting less and less effort into hiding it from the public these days. Young people usually assume that older folks are eccentric; I don't like to disappoint them. I find that others are friendlier and more interested in me since I don't mind being fallible in front of them. My quirkiness means that they can be quirky too. Ordinary is boring. It takes the pressure off everyone and as a side benefit, it makes for many shared laughs. Taking care of business is one of the joys of life; don't forget to play with it while you competently handle whatever is in front of you. I have realized that I have become more creative, less inhibited and very accepting of the uniqueness that others have as a result. More gets done. My work is better, my girlfriends are happy, life is good. My staff sends its highest regards to your staff.

SUSAN V. DARDEN

Reruns

Chapter 14

I don't watch as much TV as I did at one time in my life. I do however; have a couple of favorite shows and I find it incredibly disappointing when I make an effort to tune in only to find that I have already seen that episode. Life can be like that. You think you are all ready for something new, to move on to the next phase of your life, all prepared for it to be different this time. After a very short while, you realize that you have been here before…it's a rerun. Not even an episode you enjoyed the first time, either. In fact, I find that the only reruns I usually catch are the episodes that were my least favorite the first time.

Most of us have heard the saying that the definition of insanity is "doing the same thing over and over, expecting different results." It's like watching a rerun and expecting the ending to be different, that is just not going to happen. Déjà vu in a life experience is an opportunity to do what your higher self knew was right the first time but your ego wouldn't let it happen. The clue phone is ringing and I think it's for you. The clue phone rings just about the time you think you are past an experience that had some traumatic effect or life-changing outcome. Answer it; tell them to take you off their call list.

Lessons we fail to learn completely the first, second, and even third time we were presented with the opportunity, will continue to pop up in our life until we get it. Not just, "oh, I get it," but "THANK YOU DEAR GOD, I GOT IT THIS TIME." Turn off your TV, step away from your monitor, run do not walk the other way as fast as you can.

If it didn't work the first time, the second time, the third time; after crying, dying, praying, polling your friends, doing all manner of self destructive things to yourself, begging, pleading, and disrespecting your boundaries; what in the hell makes you think that this time is going to be different?

My favorite excuse is "love." BUT I LOVE HIM. The blanket excuse for putting the "welcome, please wipe your feet," sign back on your forehead. Let's look at that closer. When you love someone, do you do things that you know upsets them without regard for their feelings? Do you walk away (either physically, emotionally or both) when they need you most? Do you say, "I love you" and act in an unloving manner? Do you lie to them, cheat on them or steal from them? Do you greet their open heart with a closed one of your own? Do you make them try to guess what the "right" thing to say is? NO.

Your head is talking to you and it is lying its' ass off. The person you say you love *does* these things. You don't *love* them; you want your *fantasy* back. You want to watch TV. Reality is too hard, it's unfamiliar after so long on a steady diet of fantasy; it's so much nicer to live in a fairy tale sometimes. Sometimes we work very hard keeping a fairy tale alive long past its prime. It may not be fun, but it's familiar so we do it again and again.

Love is knowing that no matter what happens or how ugly it gets, you can count on that person being there. Love does not flee or hide. Fear runs away or hurts and maims. Love is not high drama. Love is calm and dependable, peaceful and strong. You don't have to poll your girlfriends and reference psychology websites to help you figure out what is going on. If love were a TV show, it would be a light comedy, not a suspense thriller. You would know that the sequence of events will be gentle and palatable, touching and fulfilling before they ever play out. Someone's head will not arrive in a box via UPS the next day. When someone loves you, they are nice to you and make you feel good. When someone wants to hurt you, they make you cry and help you grow your character defects to the point where they can kill you of their own volition. Love in disguise can make you act like your own worst enemy. Love makes you better than you were before, not weak and emptier and dangerous to yourself.

We tell people how to destroy us then wonder how they knew just what to do to bring us to our knees. It was in the first airing of the episode. We reconcile with someone who has proven themself unworthy of our love with the stipulation that they "never do it again" (whatever "it" was). They already saw the first run. They know how to hurt you. You just made yourself completely vulnerable to someone who has proven they cannot be trusted with your heart. The next statement you will likely make is, "I just don't understand why this keeps happening to me." So when are you going to pick up the phone? The ringing is really getting on my nerves.

The progress in technology over the years has made drama and suspense thrillers and fantasy adventures so much a part of our daily life we expect high intensity in everything. Guess what? Life is supposed to flow gently most of the time. There will be times in everyone's life that are dramatic enough without inviting your own personal, life sized evil action figure into it. Love makes what was good better and what was bad better. If you love someone that makes the good parts worse and the bad parts terrible check yourself, you may be living out the dramas you have come to expect from watching TV and movies. Real life shouldn't be like a soap opera most of the time. You are the only one that can control the genre of your regular viewing. The remote control is in your hand.

When you spend years dealing with theatrics in your heart and life, it's very hard to adapt to the peacefulness that comes after it stops. We are creatures of habit. We gravitate to the familiar. We gripe about reruns but sit there and watch them anyway. Even when we know how they end. Change can be achieved only after awareness comes. Make being honest with yourself even more important than being honest with others. The latter can only be achieved when the former has already been done anyway.

LIFE AFTER HAIR COLOR

The best thing about reruns is that eventually they end. There will be a new season, new episodes to lose yourself in. It only seems that there will never be anything new to watch again. There will be. Direct a few episodes of your own, but go gently…life playing out is its own drama and comedy.

SUSAN V. DARDEN

Out of the Box

Chapter 15

When our country was young, we forged alliances out of our common needs and joined forces on a community level to raise barns together or make fast work of the most intricate quilts and most overwhelming harvests. These gatherings were intended to make big jobs more manageable for the individual in need but also served as social interaction opportunities. Church on Sunday was as much a chance to say hello to all your friends while you enjoyed a picnic lunch on the lawn after the service as it was to worship your God. Often these people had built the church that they worshiped in together. Saturday shopping in town was a social event, and was looked forward to all week.

The world has gotten very technical, busy and crowded over the past couple of hundred years. We have become an instant gratification society that routinely tosses out what is obsolete or damaged to get a new one rather than fix or maintain the old. The divorce rate is staggering. If your house doesn't meet your needs, you move. A storage building is trucked to your house as often as one is built on site. Irrigation systems and lawn care companies take care of chores that would have been "play time" to those who constructed our country.

The number of cell phones everywhere I go constantly amazes me. Everyone is talking to someone, yet many people seem to live much of their lives alone. In the early days of my working life, if someone requested a copy of something they expected to see it within a few days. The email request now comes from a meeting in progress in which the participants expect you to fax the document from your computer to theirs within the next few *seconds*. I often realize that I have my hand in a box of cereal or crackers impatiently waiting for the 3 minutes it takes to microwave dinner. Coffee makers are equipped with a "brew interrupt" so that you can swipe a premature cupful from an already fast brew time. Fast, cheap and easy has become the demand of the consumer.

The first winter after I left my husband my parents surprised me by buying a computer as a Christmas gift. I was touched and thrilled by their generosity. They were concerned about how much I was going out, which was about to slow down anyway, since I had quickly discovered that almost ten years away from the nightclub and singles scene had not changed it much. I was in my early forties (and had changed *a lot)* and was not nearly as entertained by loud music, drinking and the "primp and pose" routines of my earlier years. The caliber and motivations of men met under those circumstances led to quick endings of relationships that never had a chance to begin. My parents thought that a computer to occupy my time when not working would be far "safer" than being out so much. The world has indeed changed. A life in a box.

I had been a long time computer user but the internet experience was very new to me. I was fascinated and took to it like a fish to water. I had always been an avid reader and had a natural curiosity that overshadowed my lack of knowledge. I dove into this new world with enthusiasm and wonder. Within months of surfing the net and browsing the features of my Internet Service Provider, I was more than just savvy…I had become a chatter. What a concept, a party on demand. A life with a switch. A flirtation device with outward respectability. *Nerdvana.*

I "shopped" chat rooms for a while, spending a few minutes in a variety of them but kept coming back to one in particular. I quickly became a regular. It was a group of people all in their forties to early fifties. It was almost like being at a party, only no one could see you and you typed instead of talked. I quickly picked up the chat lingo, and learned about the colorful fonts, the flippant remarks, and trading pictures. I was a natural, having always had a quick sense of humor and was a fast typist. This new world was a great outlet for me. It seemed to me that the relationships I was forming with my fellow chatters were deeper and more satisfying than any I had had in a long time.

SUSAN V. DARDEN

It was very good for me to spend time with people who had similar interests, remembered the same music, found the same jokes funny, and many times were going through a divorce or had already finished their divorces. There were couples too, some had met online, and others were members of two computer households and had made this their "date" night. Just as in "real" life, relationships were formed on all levels. There were fellow chatters that drew you in immediately with their charisma and those who repelled you instantly with their crudeness and any flavor you can think of in between.

I would come straight home from work and eat dinner in front of the computer as I learned graphics online, joining special interest groups who traded their work and sometimes just interesting things they had found on the web. I became more and more involved in "my" chat room as each time I joined the group I was warmly greeted and sometimes even "summoned" in when I had signed on for the night. I "belonged" somewhere. It mattered to some whether I was there or not. That feeling fills a very primal need in all of us. On the few occasions that I deviated from my routine, I would sign on later to find emails from people wondering where I was. It would make me smile. It didn't feel like I mattered as much in my real life as I did in my cyber one.

This medium quickly overshadowed the TV at my house. My cats would often reach up and pat my arm softly with their paws, meowing as if to remind me that there was still life in our apartment. I would stroke them until they became bored with my absent-minded attention, never taking my eyes off the screen or my right hand off the mouse. The computer became my major source of entertainment and social interaction. I stopped reading books, stopped doing needlework, only used the TV as background noise, seldom went out and when I did go out I rushed to get back to my new best friend, the computer. I even checked my email at lunchtime, using checking on the cats as an excuse to go home. Two years later, after both dear old ladies had passed on, I was still going home at lunch to check emails, painfully aware that they were now gone.

I made the same mistakes that are made in the "real" world. I trusted a little too fast in some cases, was thoughtless and caused hurt in others. Miraculous things happened too though; I found a handful of friends that are like family to me. Not many that have survived the past three years, but then I realize that they would not be nearly as treasured by me, were they more numerous. I was encouraged to do things that most in my "real" life found frivolous and a waste of time. I won recognition by winning contests in graphics, satisfying a lifetime longing I had to be "artsy." I would never have tried had it not been for an online friend insisting I join him in a class. I was told by a fellow chatter that an email I had written him read like poetry, so why did I not style it that way? I had always loved writing but no one had ever called me poetic. I wrote several poems and had a few published on the web. My two dearest *eFriends* are official proofreaders of this book. They said this accountant was a writer and it became so. They gave me permission to be myself. If you are ever stuck for what to give someone, try that…you will never be forgotten by the recipient.

The biggest downfall of this whole experience is that I came to depend on it too much for my social interactions. After one rather serious relationship that had its origins online suddenly ended after much emotional trauma, turbulence, travel expense and emotional effort it dawned on me that I had very little going on in "real time." Even sunshine burns if you get too much. Someone wrote that in a poem that was popular in the 1970's. Everything old is eventually new again. New medium, same behavior, same problems. I had to learn to become "cordless" again. At least "rechargeable."

I believe that the internet is a miracle. How else do you explain someone having the vision to create such a phenomenon? How do you take a big, fast world and make it feel communal once again? In my church recently the pastor said, "God does not call the qualified, He qualifies the called." *Exactly.* The Big Guy (He lets me call Him that) knew there were all these people who needed to get a life but wouldn't because they were so spoiled by the life they were trying to achieve that they needed to be able to go buy themselves a life in a box. The world became so big, so fast, the only way we could meet all the people we were intended to encounter was to have the computer as a resource. No longer were we small communities, learning from those around us, falling in love with those we went to school with. We are driving down the interstate talking on the cell phone on the way home to watch cable TV until we go to bed only to repeat this the next day. There was a need, someone was "qualified", and it was done.

Don't get me wrong, the internet is not just for chatting. I myself, use it for everything from banking to recipes and all manner of personal, business, writing references, hobby and even medical information. It is an incredible tool. I am mainly referring to those that find it to be a low maintenance alternative to having an actual life. That included me for a while. It's a safe place to hide out while you lick the emotional wounds of the real world. The thing that is important to remember is there are others aboard who are recuperating, as well. You need to have more in common with someone than hiding from your life. This is not the case with everyone online, but I found it to be a very sad common denominator many times. It's also easier to focus on someone else's problems than your own. At the time, we think we are doing something good for someone else. Being a complete human being is the best gift you can give anyone, especially yourself.

Through trial and error, I am finding a niche for the internet in my world. As a supplement, not as the whole enchilada. While I am the first to say that I have no regrets in any of the experiences I have had online, there is no substitute for warm, personal, in-person, daily interaction. There are online symbols for hugs and kisses, but nothing feels as good as real arms around you. Many hearts have been broken because of the distance obstacle, including mine. Sometimes no matter how much you want to turn your world upside down and move to wherever your heart is, life happening keeps that from occurring. Interestingly enough the most successful relationships I have seen online, resulted in the couple going "offline." I am always glad to see that happen, it's too easy to neglect what is going on in your own house when you live in cyberspace. I can only assume that by their disappearance they have succeeded in building a "real time" life.

It is wonderful to read about dolphin watching on the internet. The pictures and now sometimes even video streaming makes it almost feel like you are right there. Except you can't feel the wind in your face, or smell the salt in the sea spray, or catch the glisten of silver gray in the sunshine as the dolphin breaks the waves and quickly slips back into the green blue water. You miss waiting for the boat to leave, getting to know your shipmates, wondering if you have the right ones in case of emergency. You miss the camaraderie of returning safely from your journey, breathless, sunburned, and giggly from the excitement of what you have experienced together. You miss the "juicy" part. Life has many dimensions. Some say there are three. I have four in my life. I am a lucky woman.

I am grateful to know that my heart is such that I have laughed and cried with those I have never met. I spent one of the best New Year's Eves of my life in a private chat room with approximately twenty people I could honestly say I loved. We laughed, drank, joked over each other's impaired typing abilities (threatening to issue CWIs…computing while intoxicated) chatted until dawn, and remembered the experience fondly for months. I have felt connected more than electronically to the pulse of the heart of humanity. I cannot and will not give up all of my life for it, but it is very much a part of the one I have. It has helped me become the person I am today just as much as anyone or anything in my real life.

I learned that no matter where or how you meet people, they are the same. There is truth and deception, love and hate, laughing and tears, open hearted souls and closed minded people…they are your neighbors, your coworkers, your family and your friends online and off.

I personally do not chat very much anymore. That served a very valuable purpose for me on my life's journey and I plan to revisit it from time to time again. My recent experiences have left me bored and wondering why I was there. I don't believe that something remains constantly valuable to your development. There is a continual evolution in your personality, don't make the mistake of doing what you do because you have always done it.

I realized recently that I didn't want a person in my life who would spend a sunny weekend in a chat room waiting for life to drop on him, and I didn't want a person who would want a person that did either. There is so very much to sample in this world of ours. I think my online experiences have made me brave enough to seek out what I want, with or without company. Good experiences leave us better than when we started, I would call this a very good experience.

One of the poems I wrote because of a fellow chatter's encouragement follows, even though it was a very early effort of mine, I still can't say it better; it definitely expresses exactly how it was.

SUSAN V. DARDEN

You Touch Me

You touch me in places
never reached before.
Through this new world, I explore with you, my special friend.
The one I let peek inside my deepest thoughts
and greatest hopes.
Without the defenses I wear in my daily life.
The life I live without you
but so very much in your light.
You touch me in a way that satisfies my hunger
like no other has before
or ever will again.
There are no rules in this new dimension.
That might be why we are so brave.
Mistakes can't be made if there are no rules
to break.
So we bare our souls and boldly try things
we never dreamed were possible,
and become each other's hero.
Touching in a way that will never be forgotten
and leaves us changed forever.

Learning to Be a Woman
Chapter 16

I remember when I first realized my parents were only human. I can't speak for anyone else, but I know for me, it was a pivotal moment in my life. I have the same chance of making good choices as they did. I have the same right to choose poorly, as long as I take full responsibility for the consequences. Just because one of them said something, did not necessarily make it true in my life. There was a certain amount of freedom in gaining that tidbit of information. It helped me write my own permission slips. Sometimes we have a hard time giving ourselves permission to do what we want or need to do. Knowing that the choice you make based on your inner voice has a better chance of being right than even what your Mommy told you is one of the milestones of life. Even white knights need a leg up now and then to make it back onto their horse.

SUSAN V. DARDEN

I was always eager to please as a child. I was basically happy outwardly, my father adored me and to this day I am somewhat a "Daddy's Girl." I remember the day he took me on a drive to tell me he was going to Vietnam, he hadn't even told my mother yet. I sat in the car in stunned silence as I tried to imagine a whole year without him in my daily life. He had been gone that long once before when I was around two, but I didn't remember much about it. This time I was eleven and I knew that it wouldn't be easy for any of us, not to even mention the fact that he would be in danger. Even though he was a career military man, his position in communications ensured that he came home most nights except for occasional temporary duty assignments. I looked forward to that very much every day.

My mother loved me too, as she does today; I have no doubt about that. She is German by birth. My parents met just after the Korean conflict, in her hometown of Otterberg, Germany. My dad's friend rented a room from her aunt. She was a young divorcing mother of a three-year-old son, who my father would adopt; working as a weaver in the town textile factory. I was born in Germany, at my Oma's (grandmother's) three-room flat with the bathroom down the alley, in the same bed that my brother and mother were born in, delivered by the same midwife, in 1956.

I think it is often easier for a father to accept his daughter as an individual than it is for a mother because there are no preconceived notions related to gender. He doesn't see himself in her as much as the mother does. I believe very strongly that even though we may be closer to the opposite sex parent as a child, we learn how to be a woman from our mothers. I know in my case, I love her every bit as much as I love my father. He just makes it easier to show it openly sometimes. The acceptance level is higher from both sides in our case. I accept him freely and he does me. My mother and I tend to see ourselves in each other. It's difficult to show your love to someone who embodies who you are sometimes.

My mother believes that to be a good woman you have to sacrifice yourself to your children, marriage and home. I believe that to be a good woman you have to be a complete person before any of those things matter. I learned my approach after trying hers for years and not liking the way it felt. The more I tried to fix and do and control, the more out of control and frustrated I felt. My father has usually acted as though I were already perfect with no outside intervention, once I got past the "scary" ages of about fourteen to eighteen. I don't feel the performance pressure from him that I feel from her.

I was a dreamer and sometimes still am. I preferred my own company to that of other children, usually involved in some fantasy whereby I would become the character in the latest book I was reading, or on a TV show that I had recently watched. I remember galloping around the playground with a scarf on my head, pretending it was a mane and I was Windy of Chincoteague, running wild and free on Assateague Island. My Barbie lunchbox was converted into a medical kit and I would wrap my dog in Ace bandages, pretending I was a veterinarian and he was recovering from some horrible accident. Mom would buy me Suzy Homemaker toys and try to get me to look "pretty" so that I would be a good little woman and be prepared for life. I usually describe myself as shy as a child, but I really don't think that it was shyness that made me hold back on being assertive with my life early on. I learned that to take the tried and true path was "safer" and that approval from others, at least from my mother, would come from conforming.

I was fascinated with the written word. Even as a five year old, I would sit at the pink desk my father had painted to match my room and copy newspaper headlines, taking them to him and slowly sounding out the words. He would beam with delight and compliment me. He would lie in bed with me at night before I went to sleep, letting me read to *him* as soon as I was able to. They bought me books and I could even read in German, devouring the story books my grandmother sent from Germany. My mother would count out dimes to buy the latest Nancy Drew mystery for me when money was scarce for luxuries, because she knew that they meant a great deal to me.

I had every doll of the moment, new clothes when she didn't get any, and her fierce defense if anyone tried to hurt me. My mother's sense of self-worth has come more from what she did for others than for who she allowed herself to be. Her mood has suffered much for that fact over the years. She is often negative and "difficult." Something done other than her way is "wrong." She doesn't understand how I have come to make most of the choices I have made in my life. I sense that she envisioned a very different kind of life for me. I have no doubt that she always has wanted the best for me. Her acceptance level of what it actually turned into is not always good. I am not a five-year-old hungry for approval anymore, I am a grown woman and I have learned the hard way what does and doesn't work in my life. I have enough silver in my hair to honestly say, I have earned the right to do this my way now. I can still turn into her when I least expect it, though and have to snatch myself back from the early lessons I learned. I have the same passionate conviction to my version of life's truths as she does to hers. We anger each other far too easily most times, recognizing in each other the rigidity that holds us back more than is warranted. Her hand comes out of my sleeve when I get dressed in the morning.

I recently rediscovered some Barbie clothes she had made for me when I was a child. I sold all my Barbie dolls and accessories many years ago. She was appalled when she heard that. I told her that they live forever in my memory, I can "see" each one very clearly in my mind's eye, but they served no purpose in my life so I let them go. Their collector value was such that I recognized the waste of them deteriorating in the attic.

I kept the Barbie clothes that my mother made, however. She had stayed up late many nights sewing or knitting the most intricate, beautiful clothes for my dolls. She had taken an old pearl necklace and used the pearls as buttons on tiny sweaters and dresses that she knit by hand from the finest yarn. She had found a faux fur cloth with a short soft pile and made coats with dresses to match the perfectly hand sewn linings. Tiny hats and purses were fashioned to coordinate with each outfit. As I removed each beautiful garment from the tissue paper I had carefully wrapped them in, tears slid down my cheeks.

She told me once that she wanted to be a seamstress but had to work at the factory instead, then she married and had babies and that would never be. There in that box, is the proof that she *is* a seamstress and she did a work of passion and love for her daughter. I had never seen the clothes in that light. I had instinctively kept them, originally out of loyalty, now out of pure love and appreciation of not only who she was, but also who she is today. As a child, I preferred the clothes that were purchased for the dolls; they were among the items that I sold. They meant little to me. The clothes she made for them will remain in my possession until I die. I have her best work with me forever, inside of that box and most of all, inside of me. She had her dreams, too.

So what about all the mixed messages of disapproval alternating with possessive love all these years? I still get those messages today. When I am thin, I should gain weight. When I am single, I should marry. When I marry, he isn't good enough and I should divorce. When I divorce, I am a fool for having given up what I worked so hard for. I let him off too easy, who will take care of me now, she won't be around to do it forever. I have been self-supporting from a very early age; it makes me furious for anyone to imply I need "taking care of." She knows this and I believe we dance some strange dance of control when we have these conversations. She is seldom pleased by what I do or who I am. *Because she is not pleased by who she is.* She should be. She raised a good woman. No matter what path I choose, it is met with disapproval, either unspoken, but clear from her body language or outright, demeaning criticism. I just want her to accept me and be happy for me, to allow me my birthright as a valuable human being with a unique contribution to make. She wants to, but she is afraid that I will be disappointed and dissatisfied the same way she was. I want the same for her, and I have the same fears as well. I want a life of "enough," she wants me to have "more." So we dance.

I watch her now and I feel pain for her instead of for me. She is very loved by my father, my brother and me. We hardly know her. She barely recognizes us. She is in perpetual motion, cooking, shopping, doing, fixing, and working. There is never enough in her world. She hoards things trying to fill a hole that has no bottom. Her house resembles a flea market shop. Even though she regularly sells or gives things away, it stays full and cluttered because she is constantly trying to bring home a "feel good." No one can do anything to please her. Not even what *she* does pleases her. I seldom hear a positive word from her, about anything. My father is quiet and withdrawn, having given up trying to make her or himself happy years ago. He has surrendered to the negativity.

I love them both beyond all descriptive words. I hurt for them the same way. There comes a time when you have to move on from the time it was your parents' responsibility to provide happiness and approval to you and finish the job yourself based on the needs that you recognize now. I am grateful for all the good things that they brought into my life, there were many then and there are many now.

I remember when I was married; it occurred to me that I was becoming my mother. My heart was poisoned by my own negativity.

I was so hurt and disappointed by the sequence of events. Resentful of the sacrifices I had made and disillusioned that these sacrifices were not being reciprocated. Nothing went right, nothing was ever enough. Nothing that I did or my husband did made me happy. I did not have the skills to turn this situation around. I worked myself into a frenzy trying to love a man the way I *thought* he should be loved rather than the way he *needed* to be loved. I had never learned how to be any different. The focus was on the *lack* in the relationship and not on the *abundance*, as it should have been. As a result, there was more lack and less abundance. It fell in ruins. I had not actually seen anyone have a successful relationship. Now I am practicing on myself. I hope to get it right one day. I *expect* to get it right one day.

I tried to do more to get more. My mother's tennis shoes smoke. She can work a 35-year-old woman under the table at the age of seventy-two. I was on that path, too. That was all I knew. I was exhausted and burned out by the age of forty-five. I have a real life model to prove that it doesn't get any better with time unless you stop doing what doesn't work at some point.

The only thing I want for my parents is to see them happy. I relate very much to how they must have felt about me all my life. Life truly does come full circle. I am convinced that my way is more palatable than theirs is, the same way they must be convinced that I am out in left field somewhere. I feel maternal and want to soothe their hurts and disappointments. I know there have been many. I have decided that I would rather be happy than be right.

My Porsche

Chapter 17

One of the most memorable gifts I have ever received in my life is packed in with my Christmas decorations. Once a year I experience the warm recollection of the first time I read the note from my friend, Lisa, written inside of a Christmas card she sent me in 1983. Lisa and I had been friends for a number of years in the 1980's. It was a trying time for her. She was married to a much older and very controlling man, was a recovering heroin addict and alcoholic, gave birth to her two daughters during that time, took her GED, got a job in an office and generally grew as a human being by leaps and bounds during the time I knew her. She was in her mid-twenties, I was a year or two older. Her courage and resilience inspired me and made me want to be more than I was. I'm still trying to grow up to be like Lisa. Willows bend so they seldom break…that was Lisa.

She sent me a card one Christmas with a note that said she had never bought me a gift because nothing seemed to be just right for me. She said that I had given her so much of myself, she really wanted to get me a Porsche and nothing less seemed enough. I laughed when I read it. Every year I re-experience the warm fuzzy glow of her love and friendship. I always thought she gave me more than I gave her. I wanted to buy *her* a Porsche.

She and I had planned a fantasy trip to the grocery store in a Porsche. We would get out of the car, and go inside in our jeans and tee shirts with a full-length fur coat casually thrown around our shoulders, pick up a package of baloney and pay for it with a hundred dollar bill, then casually stroll out. We figured that would cause the ultimate jaw drop. We would laugh heartily when we spoke of this fantasy; the uninhibited, joyful, juicy, "life is good" laugh of true friends. I don't know where Lisa is or what she is doing these days, life moved on for both of us. She lives in my heart forever and I live in hers.

It was always easier for me to be the giver than the receiver. Over time, I have learned that both are born of generosity and both are gifts that you give to *yourself.* I would usually refuse offers of help, only allowing minimal assistance from others when I knew I was in a position to either pay for it, or reciprocate in some way. I had learned over time that my independence gave me a sense of control over my life. Autonomy was something that validated me as a person and made me feel strong and competent. I didn't like "owing" anyone anything.

I found myself in a very vulnerable situation about a year ago. I was almost a thousand miles from home, knew no one in that city except the person I had gone to visit, who ended up in the hospital with a life-threatening illness. This person's family offered no support beyond dropping me off at a hotel near the airport, making it clear that I was expected to leave, even though they knew that I was more than just a casual friend to this individual. He had told everyone that I was the woman he wanted to spend his life with. A very unloving situation was about to become one of the most loving experiences of my life.

I called two friends, both "online" friends. I felt very lost and very alone. One of these people was several hours away in driving distance. Neither had ever met me in person. Every vision of a knight on a white horse riding to the rescue could not explain how this person took charge and parted the dark clouds for me. He showed up in a black Crown Victoria that would not shift to reverse. It was a white horse to me. I was taken care of and supported in a way that made me feel safe, loved and brought my own inner strength back. He came to me and took care of me with openhearted determination and willingness to participate. My money was no good while he was with me. He participated in the traumas of the moment, passing paper towels to a blubbering mass of fear, shock and self-pity, often before the tears even fell. He left only after he had made sure my immediate needs were met and I was strong enough to stand without him. He called me *his* hero before he left.

The other friend was further away and kept me under her watchful eye by telephone. She offered to wire money. I had no transportation and the hospital was a sixty dollar a day trip from the hotel. My mental state was such that I didn't trust myself with a rented car; I was a wreck and didn't want that to manifest itself on property that didn't belong to me. She offered to send me plane fare. I had called about an early flight home but decided not to go because the lowest fare was over a thousand dollars. I was glad, because it was one of those situations that just needed to play out. I wouldn't ever have been satisfied by going home. That would have been giving up. I felt the need to dig in. Her phone was a lifeline to me, keeping a thread of sanity in place while the pain and drama unfolded around me.

The lesson I learned from all this high action drama was that receiving love and support leaves you in no way indebted to true friends, and that *receiving* an honest, heartfelt helping hand is a gift in its own right. I remembered Lisa and how she empowered me by receiving my love and support. David and Sandy gave me two priceless gifts when they were there for me, the gift of assistance in my time of need and the even greater gift of my *receiving* their unconditional love. I want to buy three Porsches now. I am so glad you bought this book.

When you never allow someone else to help you or love you in your time of need, you miss a chance to experience a part of life that is very important. I do not believe that true intimacy can be achieved without receiving as freely as you give. I felt that a light bulb had come on in the pitch darkness when I realized that. I had missed many opportunities in my life to experience the depth of real love and acceptance because of my strong determination not to "owe" anyone anything. My denial of receiving love snatched me away from the very thing I craved the most…intimacy.

Receiving at that level put me in a state of humility. Constantly giving or keeping score never took me there. Humility is where I needed to be to allow the true depth of spiritual growth to take place that I was so hungry for. I wasn't such a big, strong autonomous being after all, and the surprise of it all was…I liked it. There was another kind of power in the release of the pressure of feeling that I didn't need anyone. The connection that is felt to those who see you at your worst yet *volunteer* to be with you at that time cannot be surpassed. Now I understood why Lisa wrote the note.

This life-changing lesson has taken me closer to my higher understanding of myself. The place where the Big Guy and I work together. I have recently discovered why I have had to work so hard at meditation and inner discovery. I was able to meditate after much practice and concentration, fighting off the grocery list that would pop into my head or the "should haves, could haves, would haves." After learning about humility, I was able to utilize what would turn out to be a big part of the answer for me. Instead of churning the longing for spiritual understanding inside of myself, I needed to release it to leave the boundaries of my heart to do its work. For me, a higher understanding of myself has come from the state of receptivity.

My prayers had only been requests in the past. Now and then I would say a "thank you" prayer, but usually they were about "I want."

I realized that all the truly intimate experiences in my life were about allowing love to happen to me. They were about opening my heart to what was outside of it.

My meditation and prayers are now focused on receiving the instruction from the Big Guy. "Show me." "Guide me." "Help me see it." "What can I do to make it happen?" Instead of trying to cook up an answer from inside of me, I release and ask to be shown and told. The answer comes. I ask that the God in me be allowed to go into the world to do whatever needs to be done. I do not focus on what I want for me; only good is ever intended to come to me, so why waste the energy on it. By letting my higher self (the Big Guy in a Susan suit) out into the world, a space is open for the Big Guy in a David, or Lisa, or Sandy suit to come in. That's what makes my world go around.

When someone tries to do something for you, say "thank you." Let them love you. The Big Guy likes to change clothes often; you never know whose clothes He is wearing today and no matter what He drives up in, it will look like a Porsche to you.

Enough

Chapter 18

I am a spoiled brat. I hate admitting that, even though I made the commitment to myself long ago to be honest with myself at all costs. A sense of entitlement grew inside of me over time, partly because I never really lacked anything crucial I needed to sustain my life. Knowing that fact didn't stop me from focusing on the lack in my life. Even though material things seemed to flow to me fairly easily, I seemed to always want something; money, time, stuff, spiritual peace of mind, a man in my life, more clients, a better body, longer eyelashes, patience, a fan club, and on and on through an ever-changing lengthy list of wants.

I wondered how I could have worked so hard all my life and wound up so unfulfilled and dissatisfied with what I had ended up with. Poor me. How was it that I had lost more than a lot of people ever get in their whole lives and still didn't really *know* what it was I wanted, just that I wanted *something* different or *more* than what I had already had. I had been taught that if you work hard and do "right," everything will be as you want it eventually. That wasn't playing out for me. I read stacks of books, went to seminars, joined a church, meditated and did all kinds of things to try to solve this mystery. Still there was a whining child in my head, demanding fulfillment and attention. That was where the problem was...in my head.

About six months ago, I had a light bulb moment. I had been reading a book about the laws of attraction. I found the subject intriguing and the concept very attractive, but really wasn't expecting much in the way of life changing results. I bought the book with the idea that I would be satisfied with some understanding of the subject. The basic concept in this book was that if you focus on what is lacking in your life, more of the same would come to you. If you focus on abundance, there would be more abundance flowing in. I loved that whole idea and way of thinking. How beautifully simple. How charmingly gentle. I had devoured other books on that subject along with some about good intentions and how what you intend comes back to you embodied in experience. I looked at it as an elaboration of the "what goes down, comes around" philosophy.

That seemed too easy to me as much as I wanted to believe it all. I wanted to believe in the tooth fairy as a child, but I *knew* that Dad or Mom really snuck in and put the money in my pillow. I had become a seeker of truth, on a constant quest for "THE ANSWER." All I have to do is concentrate on what I want and I will get it. I always wanted to be like Samantha on the old Bewitched television series. Now I find out that I can just twitch my nose and get everything I ever wanted. NO. As you would expect there is a little more to it than that.

What I discovered is that there were a number of steps that I had to go through to change my way of thinking. First, I had to let go of the egotistical thought processes that allowed me to think that I knew what was best for me. That was a biggie. My brain shouted out "YES, BUT..." every single time I tried to get it to shift to the acceptance mode. You don't *know* what is best for you; you *feel* what is best for you. It took a lot of practice but I am getting better at it.

It is so easy to tell another person that the sequence of events in their life is a result of some higher order of things with an ultimately good outcome in store. Faith and philosophical thinking flow like pearls from a velvet bag when you are talking to or about someone else. Accepting that as a fact for yourself is another matter entirely. If I could do it, anyone can. I made my main ambition total and absolute acceptance that I was *exactly where I was supposed to be, doing exactly what I was supposed to be doing with absolutely every single thing I needed to do it with in that particular moment, and it was going to turn out just fine.* I am human, I kick up at least once a day to try to screw this up, but that's ok, it seems to still work. Fortunately, perfection is not a requirement in getting this change working in your life almost immediately.

We are all made of energy. If you don't believe it, think about the times that you have been negative and how it affected those around you. A snarl or bark from you can change the tone of a meeting or even the mood of your family. I remember all the times I bounced up to someone glad to see them, and was greeted with a scowl or a bad demeanor. It felt like a kick. There was an internal gasp and emotional retreat. It would take a while before I would risk reaching out again. I have also experienced the opposite. Some kind soul insisting on making me giggle when I was wearing the thundercloud of negativity over my head. Their efforts were met with resistance at first, then came the internal "damn it I was having myself a good wallow," then the eye twinkle and the snicker, then the laugh. Energy is contagious. You can buy into anyone's energy anytime you let yourself or you can give them some of yours.

This doesn't happen with a nose twitch. There is no magic here. There is a conscious *choice* to be satisfied that today is the perfect place for you. Not yesterday. Not tomorrow. *Today.* There is also a conscious choice to be satisfied that all that you need to be the best you need to be today is already at your fingertips. If you decide that the world is outside of your house plotting and scheming to make tomorrow a living hell for you, the world you walk into tomorrow is going to be a scary place indeed. I have lived this and I know it is true. Nothing is sadder than watching someone revisit dissatisfaction in their daily life. I know people who wake up each morning and decide to keep on hating the life they have rather than do something to change it. I bet you know someone like that, too. I hope it's not you.

I took on a client recently who is one of the worst businessmen I have ever seen. He has three checking accounts, all overdrawn; owes back payroll and personal income taxes that will make your eyebrows hit your hairline, and had an attitude that spoke of apathy and helplessness. I looked over his information, put it in a big box and told him that I would love to help him but given what I saw, I couldn't be sure that I would be paid. I explained that not being paid made me worry about *me* instead of *him* and that I would not be able to do my best work for him because of that. I don't allow myself to do work that I am not proud of so I made the decision to decline the assignment. To say I had inner turmoil would be an understatement. I needed the work very badly but could not see the value in working for free, that would only result in a sense of failure for misjudging potential work and the risk that came with it.

Never had I been so real, so early on with a client. It was an amazing thing. I expected him to be defensive and angry. He stood and nodded his head. We had the most incredibly productive talk about taking responsibility for daily business transactions such as putting the money for the business in the bank account instead of in his pocket, for starters. I suggested that he treat his own business with the same respect that he would treat the business of an employer. He *was* after all, his *own* employer. Be accountable for his actions, not victimized by them. I told him to call me when he was ready to do what he *already knew* was right and that I would be glad to help him once there was hope that he really wanted help, and was not just looking for someone to get him out of trouble, only to continue doing business in his shoddy, irresponsible manner.

His office employee called within days and asked me to help her install some accounting software on her computer and get her started using it. I decided to proceed with caution, I was expecting that this was a mirage. I spent three hours getting her set up to start accumulating information in an orderly manner and left. I wanted to see if I would get paid for a bill for three hours of my time before I went any further.

I sent the bill, marked due on receipt. A week passed. I was busy with other matters and brushed aside even thinking about this client. The second week passed. The third week passed. During the third week I noticed the open receivable on my books. I muttered to myself about the low lifes of the world and how I should never have gone back over there. I am such a shmuck. I need to get a job. I must be crazy, what was I thinking for God's sake. I can barely pay my bills and here I am working for someone I know is a lost cause.

Within the next few days, I reminded myself of the the new concepts I was trying to utilize in my daily life. I made a conscious decision to assume that I was going to be paid, this man was making an effort, he was going to be a very good client eventually, he had demonstrated good faith and he would do the right thing. I *felt* that there was no way this man could *not* pay me, given the honesty and fairness I had shown him. I got a call that day from the office employee. She had completed what I asked her to do, had my check for the three hours, a retainer to begin on the old work and wanted to know if I could come one day the next week and show her what to do next. Sometimes the Big Guy has to demonstrate the first few times.

I never saw His nose twitch. This is where you just say "thank you" and move on.

Coincidence you say, dear reader? I don't think so. There was no reason that this was working out except that the energy was positive or channeled in a positive direction. The intentions were good, the motives were clean; therefore, it was a go.

The same day that the employee called about the checks, I got two more calls from potential clients. One I had not heard from for almost six months, the other had gotten a brochure from me two months before. At the same time that I consciously put my intentions and focus on the first client working out, I also concentrated on how much I deserved a profitable, successful consulting practice. I reinforced to myself that I was an experienced, honest, capable, competent asset to any business that needed my services and that *I had every single thing I needed to take care of any problem that might arise or access to someone who did.* Bingo.

Not two Sundays before, I spent the morning pouring over the classifieds looking for a job in my field that would allow the flexibility to keep the few clients I had, but were inadequate to provide the funding to support me. It had been over a month since I had heard from any new prospects even though I had advertised and promoted myself at least somewhat aggressively. I very desperately needed to see some sign of progress in my endeavors. How does He do that without someone seeing his nose twitch?

There is no doubt in my mind that the reason I can produce a list of former loves who all disappointed, took advantage, ran away, deceived, lied or did some other dastardly deed is because I *expected* them to. So out into the universe goes this focus on lack of understanding, lack of love, lack of fulfillment, lack of responsibility, lack of honesty and lack of commitment…what comes back? I will give you a hint…it's *not* Prince Charming. More than likely, he would say "ribbit" and have long green legs. When you focus on what you do not want, that constitutes negative energy. Remember, focusing on lack brings *more* lack.

My mother mentioned recently that she really wished I would meet a nice person. I told her I was going to. He is on the rack, down for repairs just as I am. Probably out there figuring out why he can't meet a woman to treat him right and do what she says she is going to. We are becoming the right people and when we are the right people, we will find each other. It's very simple. I have put my intentions out in the Universe; I will accept no substitutes this time. I hope he doesn't either. If I am lucky, he will know about clover blossom rings. The Big Guy will make it happen, the timing isn't right. When it is, look out…I won't be focusing on lack this time and neither will he.

Most people I know are obligated to care for others in some way, either financially, emotionally, physically or all of the above. I hear their worries about their ability to do that. Not enough money, not enough time, not enough whatever. Think back to a time when someone cared for you. Do you remember the lack or do you remember the abundance? In all but true poverty situations, I think the response will be abundance.

I can't tell you how clean our bathroom was when I was a child, but I remember the night my Dad showed me that the toothpaste cap made a very nice flower vase for my doll house. I didn't realize the Currier & Ives dinnerware we used only on Sundays and special occasions came packaged in boxes of soap powder until I was a grownup. I begged for (and got) those very dishes for my own first apartment. They always made me feel festive and the shade of blue that those dishes are is still my favorite. I still seek out pieces at flea markets and have accumulated a large set that I love and they conjure up imagined smells of pot roast and mashed potatoes. I remember the furniture my parents bought unfinished and learning to write at the cotton candy pink desk my father painted. I remember him sitting and reading the paper while I chattered on a play phone behind him, snipping at his hair with plastic scissors in my pretend hair salon. I remember feeling inadequate and stupid sometimes and always seeing that I reflected back brilliantly in his eyes. I remember the look on his face when he was walking me down the aisle at my wedding. I wanted to run the other way. He would have let me. He would have held my dress up so I could get out of there quicker without tripping on it.

Leave your children something they will have forever. Abundance and the knowledge of where to find it. All you will ever need is within you, looking elsewhere will cause you to miss it. It is admirable if you have the money set aside for your children's college education. It is *abundant* to instill in them a love of learning and the freedom to express their passion. They will *find* a way to go to college if that is what they want. They will remember where their drive came from much longer than where the cash came from. Let them see their Mom and Dad dance in the kitchen and snuggle on the couch. If they are in a single parent household, let them see that the disappointments of what didn't work out will not keep their parent from living a full, happy and most of all, abundant life. Do not criticize their other parent, because that person is a part of them…they will feel lacking and somehow responsible for the outcome of your choices. The most important thing that any child of any age needs is a real life example of a role model living without lack in their life.

The greatest blessing you can wish on any one at any time is simply, *"I wish you enough."*

The Kitchen Is Burning
Chapter 19

Everyone who drives has experienced the knowledge that a car moving close to them in traffic is going to pull out in front of them even without that driver signaling his intention to do so. For me, a voice says something like, "that idiot is going to pull over here" right before it happens. Your heart pounds when it happens anyway, even though you were prepared. Some would chalk that up to years of driving experience, some to intuition, and some to the intervention of a higher authority. I think it is a combination of all three. An "A" team of the highest order. It takes all of them to survive.

I believe that all human beings come equipped with an internal tool kit. It contains every single skill that you will ever need to survive. Just like any good artisan, you should respect your tools and care for them well, so that they can serve you all of your life. If you ever forget about the tools entrusted to you, you will flounder, ill equipped to do what you most need to do for yourself.

In the early years of development much time and effort is spent teaching our children to walk, talk, be potty trained, and to eat independently with some semblance of grace. Later, the focus is on reading, writing, grammar, mathematics, and social protocol. What about the tool kit? How often does anyone really take it seriously enough to consciously train a child to care for the very tools that will potentially save his life and many times his heart, spare him needless suffering or cope with the times that pain is inevitable?

Young people are in the very place emotionally that would allow that sort of training. They haven't been exposed to the 1-800 numbers on TV professing that for $3.99 per minute a foreign accented person will shuffle cards and inform you of your destiny. The world is still very much "what you see is what you get." They know that the man down the street makes them feel "weird" when he looks at them, or that the dog behind the neighbor's fence will bite even though it wags its tail when they pass by. Adults often diminish these inborn volumes of knowledge without even realizing they are doing a disservice. They will encourage little Johnny to say "Hi" to the nice man, he just spoke to you; or to pet the doggie, he just wants to be friendly. This invalidates a child's instinctive feelings of their own self-pace and makes them doubt the messages that come from within. For many, years later they will address this loss of natural timing and recultivate what was automatic long ago. That is, if they are lucky, they will.

LIFE AFTER HAIR COLOR

My tool kit always beaconed me a little more persistently that most people I know. I had a rich resource of multi-cultural relatives and acquaintances and a sincere interest in the unexplainable. I have always been drawn to the unique, bold personalities of the world. The people who march to their own drum music and are often thought to be "strange" by society are the ones I am drawn to. I preferred adults as company when I was a child and was fascinated by "old wives tales" and the stories that well traveled people told. I respected wisdom as much then as I do now. I never questioned how someone just "knew" something unless the story their eyes told me differed from the one that came from their lips. I am never comfortable conversing with someone whose eyes are not visible.

I think of my great-grandmother every time I see a cardinal. I live in Virginia where the vividly red birds flock spring through fall. I get a "rush" every spring when I spot the first one of the season. As a child, I was fascinated that there were several cardinals that came to her back doorway to be fed each day. She would hear their calls from the kitchen and immediately take their meal to them; they allowed her to get within a few feet of them to deliver the goods. She would greet them warmly with cooing and baby talk as though they were her children.

I didn't realize until many years later that not everyone had cardinals at their back door or entryway. Except for the years I lived in Germany, there has been a profusion close by wherever I have lived. They jet around my parents back yard in prolific numbers. They nested in a tree outside my apartment balcony. They nested just outside of my back door at two different houses I have lived in. I have heard that there are many people locally who consider themselves lucky to see a few a year. My former husband would be amazed that I would state suddenly and confidently, "Listen, a red bird…" He would say, "How do you do that? I didn't hear a thing." He was always impressed when I called him to the window or back door and pointed out the crimson flier very close by. I don't know how I do it, I just do. I have come to just say "Hi, Annie" when I see one, I figure she is just trying to keep up with all of us. I like her there. My brother gave me a brooch last Christmas, a beautiful cardinal done in red crystals, I wear it proudly and often, it touches me to think that he noticed the cardinals, too.

I never have my hands in the earth or potting soil without the presence of my Oma (German grandmother). I accompanied her many days on her walk up the hill to the nursery she worked at part-time until she was well into her seventies. She would bend from the waist to tend rows of plants that seemed to reach for her as she nurtured them. Her tiny flat was modest but the window boxes overflowed with geraniums and multicolored flowers that announced that someone who loved them lived there. I have been reprimanded many times for bending at the waist instead of kneeling to tend plants or work a garden. It works better for me that way, the plants reach for their hugs as I work.

Oma told me that there was a time in her village when all black kittens were destroyed because they were thought to be witches cats. She and I never chose anything other than a pitch-black cat as a pet.

We never discussed why, we just took them. The only deviation from this was when we were given a cat by someone else. The ones we chose were always black. The last cat I owned chose me, she was black as well. She was my fur child for sixteen years and her face was identical to a cat owned by Oma when I was young. I have no doubt that she sits at Oma's feet in heaven now.

A well-respected psychotherapist client referred me to a "reader" after one of our many conversations about the paranormal. He was as fascinated as I was by the subject and was doing research about it. I was honored that he shared his resources with me. I went to her with an open mind and a sincere curiosity. One of the things she told me was that I was being watched over by an old man. She said that he kept up with me yet remained out of sight. She wondered aloud if it was my grandfather. I replied that my grandfather had passed on and she insisted that this man was living. We spoke of many other things, most of them beyond my understanding at that time. She kept returning to the old man. She said he was all around me in spirit and would allow himself to be seen at some time in the future. I was frustrated and at a total loss for explanation. I liked this woman and considered the experience to be a positive one in spite of the fact that I was convinced that "wires were crossed" somewhere. I figured I wasn't a very open "read" and that the problem was with me, not her. I forgot about it.

Within two years, I got a call from my father. His father, who had been unaccounted for for over sixty years had contacted him and wanted to meet us both. I immediately thought of Kay, the reader.

My heart pounded as the facts became known. He had moved to New York when my father was around three. My father's mother was young and troubled, his grandparents took over his upbringing and his father felt that it would be less disruptive and better for his welfare to just leave it at that. This occurred in the 1930s, things were handled very differently back then. He kept up with where we were and what we were doing through a network of distant relatives in the area who knew our whereabouts but they said nothing to us of the contact with him.

I met with my grandfather in person twice before he died. I don't know if it was more a miracle to me or to my own father. I am just grateful for the experience. Both meeting him and having had it disclosed beforehand. I don't know how it works, it just does.

While remodeling my house when I was married, we encountered an endless list of problems and obstacles in the process. We chose an under qualified contractor initially, who caused some serious structural damage to the house. We went through eighteen months of turmoil, exorbitant expense, inconvenience and all the problems you can imagine in the way of relationship strain, including a legal battle with the first contractor we used. My business was at home so that was disrupted as well as the household routine. My husband and I talked of little except how to get the house back together and how much it would cost. Our mortgage exceeded the value of the house at one point; we thought we would never get out from under the rubble, literally and figuratively. It would have never been completed without personal loans we took out from family.

During that time, he took numerous business trips. I knew they weren't all business, but frankly I was so angry with him for leaving this monumental task mainly for me to solve on my own, when the bulk of the project was his idea to begin with, I was often glad he wasn't around. His main input came on the financial end, critical and disapproving, yet offering no solution beyond "press on…we have to get this fixed." Things happened that didn't add up. Small events occurred over a period of time that nagged at me. I had never mistrusted him before, but I did now. One day when he returned from a trip, I burst into tears and heard myself saying, "You are giving her my *life* and I don't know why." The "her" I was referring to was the same person who wore the identical dress as me to the first company party we attended, the same person who would listen to his frustrations about what home life had become and buy him golf lessons for his birthday, innocently explaining that she only wanted to make him happy because she knew his life was so stressful. She offered that explanation when she heard that I had said the expensive lessons were an inappropriate gift in a business setting. I had promised him that I would get the golf lessons for Christmas; he had mentioned it at work. He only looked at me in response, stunned and pale. He knew that I knew, I could tell. He profusely denied any wrongdoing. He assured me that when the house was finished I would relax and not be so paranoid about everything. The house took a very long time to finish.

Looking back, I know now that *when you smell your kitchen burning if you let someone convince you that it's not, your house will burn down.* You know when something is wrong. The signs are all there. The house was out of control because we were out of control. The negativity and bad karma kept everything going in the wrong direction. The lies and deceit poisoned what little good intention was left. An opportunist spotted a hole in a wounded relationship and jumped through it, offering an escape to a person unequipped to deal with fighting a real life fire. This didn't happen overnight. I had a sick feeling in the pit of my stomach for a very long time. Even after I smelled the smoke, I thought that I could build a wall that it couldn't burn through. I forgot about my toolkit. It was sitting there waiting for me the whole time. I won't be forgetting it again.

When I finally walked away from that house in 1999, almost five years after I first smelled smoke, I was a newly enlightened person. I knew one thing for certain. The voice inside of me never lied. I could choose not to listen, but it never lied. It would be there, telling it like it was, whenever I would hear what it had to say. I have chosen not to listen a few times since. I am back to carrying my tools because of it.

I chose to leave a lot of myself behind there, but I took the best part with me. I had hand painted a floor to ceiling wall of windows in the great room. Each panel, nine in all plus two French doors, was frosted to let light in yet lend privacy from too-close neighbors, in the center of each I had painted a flower. There was a different flower on each panel inside of a medallion that I had designed. They resembled stained glass. It was a garden of glass. More prayers and spiritual explorations were done while painting those windows than any masterpiece in the Louvre. Every time I looked at them, I thought of the hours I spent in solitude, tapping a bent paper clip into the paint to texturize it, searching my mind for answers to the burning questions of my life. Many people suggested that I scrape it off, that leaving my labor of love for someone else to enjoy would be a crime and a disservice to me. I chose to leave it as I had planned. I took with me all that made that house a home; I left the part of the karmic debt behind that wasn't mine for someone else to pay off. I had paid my share. I drove by that house recently; the windows remain as I left them. The black-eyed susans, irises and roses bloomed profusely in the yard. I was proud. Oma would have loved seeing them there. No flower should be sacrificed in pain, only in joy.

On the morning of September 11, 2001, I was at my desk at work. Everyone was listening to the horrible accounts of the first plane striking the World Trade Center. I was as shocked as anyone, speechless and stunned that such evil could penetrate the physical boundaries of what I felt was the safest place in the world to live. Suddenly I felt the most incredible emptiness. It was as if the entire world stopped. The wind was knocked out of all humanity. There was an abyss of agony and despair inside of my heart that I had never experienced before. It was as if a person opened their mouth to scream but no sound came out. Only the agony and horror of a face stretched and contorted into a primal earth-shattering scream. Within moments, the impact of the second plane had been announced. The world had stood still for me as it happened. I remember feeling my eyes sting, but no tears fell. The pain was too great, there was only shock, then exhaustion.

In the days that followed, I grieved with the rest of the country, watching the news, being a little kinder and introspective, touched by the reminder that all any of us has is today. For months if someone would ask how I was doing, I would reply, "at least I didn't get blown up at work today." Nothing seemed very important when you looked at it from that perspective. I would usually get a somber nod in response. It was my way of lending some value to the senseless, wasteful act. I didn't want to forget and return to "normal." There was a reverence for life, not only my own, but everyone's. It changed me forever. It amazes me that it didn't change every single person in this country. I assumed early on that it had, I have come to see that that is far from the truth.

I have discussed the feeling I had with several people since the event. I was not alone that day. There were many who felt the horror and pain from countless miles away. There was a worldwide connection of empaths that day. I have spoken to several of them myself. A miracle was born of despair and tragedy. I hope I am always the kind of person who feels things intensely. I am not afraid of it. I believe that I am one of the lucky ones. I get the "juicy" fruit…the tomatoes that pour rivers down my arms and drip off my elbows and the peppers that squirt and sting the skin they are allowed to remain on. I like it like that.

Living Juicy

Chapter 20

Years ago, my brother had an automotive shop on the rough side of town. He made some bad choices just as we all have and it probably wasn't the best of situations. He taught me something during that time, however. He did things his way. He would cook steaks in the back of the shop with his friends after hours, on a grill made from tire rims. They would use their pocketknives to lift the meat off the grill when it was cooked to suit them and lay them on a phone book, which had its cover torn off. If there were more people than phone books, they would share. They would drink beer and laugh, not even pretending to tell the truth in the stories they exchanged. When they were through, they would "do the dishes" by tearing off the pages that had gotten soaked by meat juices and cut by their sharp knives, and toss the phone book aside to use for the next cookout. Hopefully, they wouldn't need to call anyone that was on one of those pages. The scraps went to the shop cats that were waiting behind the oil drums and in the rafters. I remember cringing when I walked up on this party a time or two. My mother would have fainted had she seen it. I can assure you, he did not learn this at her house.

Some would call the scene I described as "redneck." I don't think they cared what anyone would call it. It was men hanging out, talking and enjoying the feeling that a day's work was done as well as they could do it, cooking their food together and eating it with great enjoyment with trusted companions. Without a woman in sight, they were free to "regress." They were taking great pleasure in a simple experience. My brother referred to this ritual as "burning meat." I still smile when I hear him say he is going to "burn some meat." They were living juicy. I think that is a very civilized thing. Once you learn what living juicy is, it's very hard to settle for less. He has had bigger steaks since then, served on nicer plates to be sure. I would bet that he hasn't had many that tasted any better, though. I remember how he smiled when I would walk into this scene. I prefer my steak on a plate, but I love living juicy just as much as anyone does.

Living juicy is standing outside on a deck in the dark chilly night after getting out of a hot tub. You have the towel, but it winds up on the rail. Your skin is pink and moist from the long soaking. The cool air causes a confusion of physical sensation that is startling then calming. An awareness and presence in the moment surrounds you. The stars are your only witness. You make mental note to do this again, and soon. It's your little secret. No one saw and it revived a part of you that sleeps through your daily life.

Living juicy is an ordinary thing done exactly your way. No apologies. No explanations. No mental backlash. You have a permission slip from your internal parent to just let it rip. Total enjoyment and presence in the moment. Most of us don't allow ourselves to get juicy often enough. The best recharging of emotions and energy come from living juicy. I am learning that I don't want my life to be without it.

Feed your inner child ice cream for lunch some hot summer day. Remember how you drooled at the ice cream parlor as a child. Put everything on there that you wanted then but you weren't supposed to have. This one experience won't hopelessly blow your diet, and it will truly feed your soul. Make sure you do it again before Labor Day.

Only allow yourself to partner with a lover who dares to speak up when they think you are wrong. I have found that a relationship with an opposite sex recording of myself leaves me cold and even disrespectful of that person. I doubt their feelings for me. The opposite of love is not hate, it is *apathy.* If you don't love me enough to tell me straight up what is on your mind, leave me be. Passion flows in both directions. I try to stay off one-way streets. I'm living juicy now. The honest and fair exchange of opinions is fuel for a dazzling fire. Blind agreement to avoid the effort of communication is a death sentence to even the most carefully selected union. Don't buy into someone saying they love you but acting as if they don't.

Love doesn't need words to express itself, but words can falsely express love. Real love is juicy, you can feel it.

If you care enough for someone to want them physically, make sure you love them as if it will be the last time every time. You never know which time will be the last time. One of them will be. Living juicy means there are no regrets. If you love someone, tell them you do. You will never be sorry you did, but you will always regret it if you don't.

No matter how many times you chose a partner that ultimately hurt you or did wrong by you, listen for the "wow" that will inevitably speak from within you again. This new person never hurt you. Love them like no one ever hurt you before. Then let them love you back. Be honest with them and yourself about your fears, but don't punish them for what someone else did to you or helped you do to yourself. Risks are juicy. There is never a reward without taking a risk.

Drive to nowhere and take your time getting there. Stop when you are tired at a hotel that is not a national chain. Eat where the truckers do. Shop where there are old men and dogs sitting around the entrance. Smile when you pass them. I bet they talk to you. Look people in the eye. Some will look through you. A few will meet your eyes with their own and smile, some will even speak. The people who live juicy recognize each other and they are always glad to say hello to one of their own.

When the clerical worker who delivers the mail to your desk comes around tomorrow, look up and listen for the answer when you ask how she is. Notice something about her and compliment her on it. She will pass that favor on as she completes her route around the building. I guarantee it.

Mother Theresa was known for her compassionate acts, her humble spirit and her generous heart. She said, "We can do no great things, only small things with great love." Mother Theresa lived juicy. Maybe not the way you or I would, or could even find the strength to, but she found what made life juicy for her and she did it better than anyone else. Do what you do better than anyone else does. Especially the small things.

Don't get worried about the sand in your vehicle tracked there by beach walking feet. God made sure someone had the vision to invent the vacuum cleaner for that very reason. Be happy that there was someone to walk on the beach with you. The place where the land meets the sea and the sky is holy and it is a special gift to have someone to appreciate it with you. Hold hands while you walk there, link arms, just touch.

Listen to the stories that the old people tell. The answers are subtly disguised as ramblings in their narratives. I had an aunt whose favorite saying was "right's right but wrong's nobody." None of us knew what it meant for sure, but I mentally hear her say it several times a week. I always smile when I do. I wore one of her rhinestone chokers to a party at the Cavalier Hotel, in Virginia Beach, almost exactly fifty years after she had worn it to the same place. I felt her presence the whole time I was there. She would have liked my shoes.

They hurt, but I looked good. She liked living juicy, too. Unfortunately, I don't remember seeing her do it too often.

I remember being at a huge theme park on a very crowded day. There were rides and activities, shows and elaborately staged vignettes with costumed characters. All manner of things to do and see in a carnival atmosphere. I had sat down on a bench to cool off for a few minutes and watched a young father coax his tiny son away from the pigeons he was feeding next to the concession stand. All Dad knew was that he paid a lot of money to get the family in there, and he wanted to see some enjoyment to equal that investment of effort and recreational funds. Sonny was enchanted by the pigeons. I would have let him keep feeding them. I watched the man drag the boy away by the hand as the little fellow kept looking back over his shoulder at the only attraction that spoke to him that day.

No one can tell you what is juicy to you, only you know. Do it often and as hard as you can. Live as if you mean it, this is not a rehearsal.

About the Author

Susan V. Darden was born in Germany in 1956 to an Air Force enlisted man and a German factory worker. She traveled extensively with her family throughout her childhood, finally settling in Chesapeake, Virginia in the late 1970s. She has lived in the Tidewater region of Virginia ever since.

In addition to her writing endeavors, Susan is self-employed as a system design and accounting consultant to small businesses and individuals. She is a multi-faceted, involved individual constantly striving to learn new things and pass along her accumulated knowledge to others with a lighthearted touch. She enjoys a humorous, practical approach to most of life's challenges.

Printed in the United States
1312400002B/1-102